VISION CIRCLE

VISION CIRCLE

Shaman Dreamers of the Crystal Cave

)

Jeff Farwell

PASSAGEWAY

Passageway Publishing
PO Box 520411
Salt Lake City, Utah 84152

www.PassagewayPublishing.com
orders@PassagewayPublishing.com

PUBLISHER'S CATALOGING-IN-PUBLICATION
(Provided by Quality Books, Inc.)

    Farwell, Jeff.
      VisionCircle : shaman dreamers of the crystal cave /
    Jeff Farwell.
      p. cm.
      LCCN 2009930816
      ISBN-13: 978-0-9819735-9-3
      ISBN-10: 0-9819735-9-0

      1. Shamanism. 2. Spiritual life.   I. Title.
    II. Title: Vision circle.

    BL2370.S5F37 2009   201'.44
                        QBI09-600107

To be alive when it all seems about to end
means to be near the lifting of the veil.

— MICHAEL MEADE
The World Behind the World:
Living at the Ends of Time

Contents

Introduction

The Veil Thins

Not so long ago the veil between the worlds was almost impenetrable. Only through heroic and concerted effort was it possible to touch those realms beyond the radius of our senses and return to tell of them. Of course, there have always been thin spots and places of strange power, just as there have always been a few men and women who could reach beyond the visible. Such people have been called prophets, shamans, and insane.

That is no longer the case. We find ourselves in a time of great shifts in which many doors are opening. What was unavailable to most is now becoming accessible to all. Before us is an invitation to join a vast, multidimensional universe whose vistas and inhabitants are as tangible as we consider ourselves. We can directly access spiritual realms, wisdom, and love to experience our own timelessness and truth—if we choose. The first step in that choice is to acknowledge that we too are infinite by nature. The second and much harder is to open the eyes of the heart and trust what it tells us. The brain tells us the heart cannot be understood. Most of us have been content with this conceit and have never considered that the heart might be a potent organ of perception.

The density of the veil has even hidden us from ourselves. It is common to hear that we are powerful beings, but it is not something most of us have allowed ourselves to experience. Instead we attribute states of fear, want, and suffering to God or bad luck, failing to recognize the awesome creative power of human thought and the forms it has created and sustained for millennia. How do we step out of the fearful inertia that seems to blanket the world and the sense of helplessness it perpetuates in us all? By starting to accept our divinity as an actuality rather than a concept. Doing so, you may be surprised to find that the world shifts slightly.

Many of us feel as if time is somehow speeding up. Such is the pull of the time to come. With this shift comes both invitation and responsibility. The invitation is to glimpse in each other who we really are and who we are becoming. The responsibility is to allow that vision to open and from there to hold space for an even larger vision, one in which we dream into being a new world of beauty, compassion, and grace. We are not at the end but the beginning.

The experiences that follow came to me within my own practice of shamanic journeying and coincided with changes in my life. I did not seek them specifically and would have been happy to continue my way in a comfortable career, troubled only by an occasional feeling that I was doing a good job of skating the surface. Something activated a deeper seed. It is hard to point to a single action, event, or idea, though I can suggest many. Perhaps their effect was cumulative. Perhaps it was time. i nurtured that seed and a path slowly emerged, branching from the momentum I assumed was the course of life. Perhaps the possibility was always present, a question waiting to be asked and finally answered, a choice leading to unimagined choices.

After a few years I found the two paths had diverged enough that it would soon be difficult to keep a foot on both. I chose the one that seemed the juiciest and never looked back. It led directly to a life in which the distinction between inner and outer experience was less apparent, and there would be unfamiliar roles such as healer and teacher. The unknowns were part of the attraction, yet the path soon began to feel natural, familiar, and rich—a place I had always sought without knowing it. In a way, I think it chose me long before I made my choice.

And I had help. My journeying experiences and work with guides, teachers, and spirits in both inner and outer domains were an unfailing source of support, while challenging me to walk in a conscious, living universe filled with magic, witnessing the sacred in the mundane.

A month before I made the leap, a man of power approached me in the inner world with the unexpected invitation I had somehow been expecting. I accepted and found myself in a council of dreamers, a vision circle linked to other circles back through linear time charged with assisting the Earth and her inhabitants in times of transition. With that charge came a task specific to me: the work of the Council and some of my other encounters would form a book that I was to write and which is now before you.

There are different ways to approach this account. The easiest is to suspend disbelief and simply enjoy the story. Whether you consider it truth or fantastic tale is not really important. What matters is that it speaks to you. Allow it to open your heart and the realm of possibility. Perhaps the telling will activate your own trust in a bright future. May it give you courage to acknowledge and then step through fear to accept what calls more and more insistently.

There are no more prophets. The time of prophecy is over. We are indeed the ones we have been waiting for. The veil grows thin!

)

I offer this book with honor and respect to the Earth and her inhabitants with the simple intent of highest and best for all. Thanks are due to everyone who has assisted with its publication. I am blessed. And I offer deepest gratitude to my teachers in all worlds with the hope that in a small way this work helps further their own.

1

The Traveler

~January~
Waxing Moon in Taurus

Aquila, the great wolf and steadfast helper who led me to my first guide, told me there was someone in my valley. I got a picture of a man dressed in fur with a wolf's-head hat, moving carefully through the trees and snow.

"He hunts you."

)

There was one other time when I encountered someone in my inner domain. I knew he also walked in the Middle World, the small part of the Universe most people are satisfied to call real. Then, he too sought me but in a nonspecific way. I saw him across a stream, far from the places I usually frequented, where I had ventured while working with the protector being who has no name.

For a few days I observed that earlier intruder, knowing he could not see me though he was aware of being observed. He kept piling rocks in a heap that never amounted to much. Perhaps he considered himself a great sorcerer, entering what he imagined was the heart of someone's inner world. Curiosity finally got the better of me. With the protector close at hand I crossed the water and approached his back.

"What is your name?" I asked.

As usual he was half-heartedly trying to make the same round rocks into a structure. He wore a great, black fur coat that went well below his knees, despite the day's apparent warmth.

"Anton," he replied, without wanting to, and turned toward me.

"What are you doing here?"

"Trying to attract you."

"Here I am. What are you building?"

"A school, perhaps," he said without real conviction.

In these realms it is difficult to lie, but he attempted to keep the whole truth from me. I sensed that his larger plan was to attract people to his own purposes and that in daily life he was often a manipulator and a liar—no doubt for worthy causes. I visited him again shortly thereafter to confirm my initial impression and then abandoned him to his devices. Later I chanced to learn his earthly identity, but that is another story.

And once something strange and unbidden found its way to my inner world. It was night. I was standing on the rim of the valley when the protector, who rarely spoke, suddenly said, "Duck! Hide! Do not look up!" I immediately went small and invisible and felt a darkness full of intent fly over like a great, silent bird. It went up the valley, circled at the end, and passed over again. Then it was gone and the protector removed his cloak of shadow from me. I later asked my guide, Amun, about it.

"Sometimes things can enter," he said, unconcerned.

Perhaps he was trying not to alarm me. Whatever it was, it had malice.

)

So when Aquila, the wolf, told me I was being stalked in my own place of relative safety, I was intrigued but wary and kept my distance. I saw from the picture he gave me that this fellow was masterful. Still I was secure in the knowledge that I had numerous means of protection and refuges that remained inviolate.

The intruder made camp near the head of the valley and there he stayed. Some days I forgot all about him until I journeyed to that realm, which I had to do to see Amun. Together we observed him from our meeting place, but Amun simply said, "Watch a little longer. Proceed carefully."

Finally I ventured toward his place with Aquila and the protector. We stayed on the far side of the little stream that flows from the sheltering mountain jutting overhead, much as I had done with the previous intruder in a different place. Mirroring the seasons in my outer world, it was winter there, midmorning. The stream was frozen and snow covered. The sky was slightly overcast. I had the protector envelop me in shadow and observed this man more closely. He was dressed in white furs streaked with brown. A shaman. I knew he was aware of my presence though not my location. Unlike the earlier trespasser, he sat quietly before a small fire, open to my scrutiny, hiding nothing, alert, powerful.

Still in shadow, I crossed the stream yet he saw me coming. I released the shadow, keeping the protector close on my right. He seemed relieved and stood immediately. His face was open.

"Who are you, and what are you doing here?" I asked brusquely.

He smiled. "I am the Traveler. I am seeking you." He shifted his fur-booted feet and the snow squeaked in the deep cold.

"Why?"

"I bring an invitation. There is a cave in the Middle World high on a mountain face. It has a great crystal. Come to it." He sent me a picture: a cave in a sheer rock wall, high above a narrow valley choked with boulders and stone shards.

I liked him and could feel my insubordinate heart opening. I was in the presence of someone strong in the path and connected to Spirit. He seemed amused by my thoughts but said nothing more. I thanked him and moved back across the river into what I hoped was disappearance. When I looked down from my vantage point with Amun, the Traveler was still there, but he seemed to be fading.

Knowing my question, Amun said, "Be very careful. Use all your invisibility—if you accept."

I had been hunted successfully. There was bait. Was there a trap?

)

I planned to take my time visiting that cave. A leisurely approach would be a statement of indifference. But the next morning I knew it was the only thing I could possibly do. It felt big, and my curiosity was extreme. A little vanity contributed to the mix.

I asked Red Feather, the spirit who is connected to me in outer life and who walks on my left, if he wanted to join.

"I think it may be what I'm here for," he answered.

Beginning at my valley, we flew through the Middle World with the protector and all the invisibility I could command. Soon I was floating outside the cave mouth whose picture I saw the day before. All seemed dark within, though I could see a big, double-terminated crystal about eighteen inches long and perhaps twelve wide, one point almost buried in an alcove at the back of the cave. Then I realized there were several men and women seated along the sides. Another man sat directly beneath the crystal, which emitted a soft glow. He had seen me well before I noticed him, as did one or two more.

"Come in!" he said, startling the others who were staring at the cave floor or lost in meditation. "The Traveler found you."

I saw that the Traveler himself was seated a little to the man's right. Balanced at the lip with a thousand feet of stone face below my heels, alert for danger, yet sensing nothing but welcome and gladness from those in the chamber, I recognized a pivotal moment. Suddenly the cave seemed warmer, suffused with a rosy, golden light. Still I hesitated. Lines of possibility stretched in every direction, though there was only one choice.

"Come in," he said again. "Sit here on my left. This will be your place."

I entered. Approaching him, I saw a well-built man with golden-brown skin, a broad, unlined face open to my scrutiny, and graying hair hanging in two braids just below his shoulders. He seemed to be bare-chested, and his large turquoise aura added to the glow in the cave.

With Red Feather close behind me, I sat where the man indicated. The others watched intently. What had Amun seen to make him urge so much caution?

"Who is the Traveler?" I asked, looking at them both.

"He is helping us gather all our members. When we are complete there will be twelve, plus myself. He will not be one of us, though he will help us on occasion. All of us here are currently living lives on Earth. You may encounter some of the members in life. Others you will only meet here. My name is Arrow." He laughed as I tried to be certain he didn't have a half-dozen other names that sounded similar.

I studied the cave and those who were in it. There were three people against the left wall, three on the right, and with the Traveler, Arrow, and me, three at the back. The cave did not seem to have any exit other than the front.

"With your arrival there are now seven members, five to come, six female, six male altogether," he continued. "The Traveler is contacting the other five." As he said that, the Traveler got up, moved to the cave mouth, and disappeared into the air.

I considered the number twelve: twelve solar months, twelve astrological signs, twelve Christian apostles, twelve stones in my medicine bundle, and so on.

"All that," Arrow said dismissively. I felt myself smile. I liked very much that the symbolic was simply assumed rather than the primary object of attention here.

I had another question. "What about thirteen?"

"The thirteenth connects you with a lineage, as with the stones in your medicine bundle. That is my function. I will lead." He gave a great laugh, and I could see the lineage stretching out in time behind him for an instant.

"You are the next shamans and will each carry this lineage eventually. You are the Council. Your purpose is to dream the world into being. There may be other councils, perhaps many, but that is not our concern. One reason you are all here is your skill at manifestation."

I thought about how I'd like to manifest a few things more directly in my own life, but I understood him. Gathering courage, I looked at each person in the cave starting on my left. There sat two women and a man between. I looked at each carefully, tried to get their names and look into their eyes. With each I sensed nothing but welcome and joy at my presence. It was hard to keep them in memory. On the right side sat two men with a woman between. The man nearest the cave mouth was short, slightly stocky, with brown skin and perhaps a pencil mustache. He seemed somewhat less open than the others, and I suddenly thought "Loki" and flashed on the idea that Loki might be a necessary part of creation as well. But then I thought, "Paqo!" and a voice seemed to say, "Or someone like him." He nodded and smiled, returning my recognition. I knew this man.

The woman in the middle was African and very large. "I have to be large to hold all this joy and energy," she said, reading my thoughts and laughing.

The last man was Alfred, a tall, older man, whom I knew from some of my training. Again I heard, "Or someone like him." I felt another wave of recognition and happiness, which he returned.

"But I can think of many who are more qualified than I to be sitting here," I said to Arrow.

"Those people are engaged in other tasks of equal importance for which they are best suited. Teaching, for instance. We will soon be at thirteen, but until then we will not join hands or conduct our formal duties. To begin we will meet at each new moon. Later we may add something at the time of the full moon or as necessary, but for our immediate purposes new moons are better."

I had forgotten about Red Feather, still sitting very quietly a little back and to my left.

"What about my friend?"

"Another one of the reasons you are here. He is not currently one of those with a physical presence on Earth and cannot participate directly, but as he is directly attached to you and shares your path he may stay where he is. We welcome him. As for the rest, guides, power animals, helping spirits, and so on, all of it stays outside the cave."

Everyone laughed.

It all seemed good and very right. A few months before, I could not have imagined such a thing, let alone the idea of participating in it. I felt honored and excited but awed by the responsibility.

Only ten days ago—New Year's Eve to be exact—I dreamed I stood on a hill with God looking on the City of Life. Among other things, I stated a loose intent to write a book of one kind or another. Now it seemed one was about to write me.

2

First Meeting

-January-
New Moon in Aquarius

Between my initial visit to the cave and our first formal meeting, I returned several times. Additional members continued to arrive, some on their own, some accompanied by the Traveler. I tried to keep them straight, yet it was as if only part of their energy was there as a placeholder. I wasn't sure exactly when we would meet at the new moon, but Arrow had said to me, "You will know." On the day of the exact new moon, I noticed that the moon calendar had come off the wall. I took it as a sign.

That evening I journeyed to the place where I had met the Traveler. I knew I could go directly to the cave but chose to begin from a deeper place as a means of heightening my focus. I continued to do so thereafter. Red Feather accompanied me. Normally the valley was a place he chose not to go, as he felt it would be an honorable thing to leave one place in my life that was mine alone. He had met Amun and was deeply moved, but I never asked whether he had a guide. Once he told me the flicker was his primary power animal. That probably explained the sudden and continuing presence of red-shafted flickers announcing their presence near my house. One thing I did ask was whether he remembered dying. He didn't. This has remained a mystery for us both. I will tell more of this matter soon.

From the valley we made our way to the cave. It was dark, but we could see the cave mouth lit by firelight from within, hundreds of feet above the foot of the mountain cliff and hundreds more below the cliff crag. We entered and the men and women already present greeted us warmly. Two more soon followed, and we were twelve, plus Arrow. Those closest to the cave mouth at each side moved toward each other

7

to complete a circle. We shared a quiet excitement. Personally I felt that by virtue of being there I was competent of the work before us — at least as I understood it — and had no sense of trepidation or inadequacy. The cave was just big enough to hold us all without crowding. A small fire burned before Arrow. Behind him the large crystal stood in its alcove.

He welcomed us with a few words and got right to business.

"Take as much time as you need to see and remember each of the others here. It is very important for our work."

I still sat at Arrow's left, but others had shifted as newcomers arrived. Except for Arrow and me, male and female alternated. I began with the person on my left, a small, olive-skinned woman with streaks of silver in her thick, dark hair. She wore a purple or black dress. Next was a rather tall man of Chinese appearance, dressed in plain trousers and a short-sleeve shirt as if he had just gotten off his bicycle in Shanghai. On his left was a white-haired woman wearing what appeared to be a white buckskin dress with beaded symbols. Next to her was a short, somewhat stocky man with dark skin and black hair in a bowl cut, an Amazonian shaman. He had red paint in lines across both cheeks and around his right upper arm. And then a surprise — at least Arrow had told me it might be a surprise during one of my intervening visits. I do believe it was Alice, a large woman with short, dark hair, wearing a long dress of blue or purple. Her back was most directly to the cave entrance; something I realized was not by circumstance.

Continuing around was Paqo, "or someone like him," a Peruvian shaman I had met several times and who was probably the youngest person there. Then came the large African lady with the beautiful face, then Alfred. After him sat a tall, thin, northern European woman with high cheekbones, gray eyes, and long blonde hair streaked with gray. She wore a white shirt and black pants. On her left sat an African man, tall, strong in every sense, so black he was almost blue. He wore a flowing robe printed with unique geometric symbols and a matching cap. And finally there was someone I had difficulty making out, partly because Arrow sat between us, but perhaps because I was reluctant to recognize someone I knew. At length, she seemed to resolve into a tall woman, dressed in radiant white with a white headband and some kind of medallion on the front. Her hair seemed short and might have been ash blonde.

Me? It is always hard for me to discern my own form and appearance while journeying, but I believe I was wearing the white buckskin medicine shirt given to me a little earlier by a group of Paleolithichunters I had met at a "thin place."

As I engaged each person, I felt my attention mirrored. In every case we looked within each other's eyes and recognized something common that manifested simultaneously in a warm smile.

I do not know if Arrow was waiting for me, but at that point he said, "Good. We have work to do. You are all currently living on Earth, as am I. You are here because of your abilities at manifestation and because it is your self-chosen destiny. There may be other groups engaged in the same work, but for us this is the only one that matters. If you notice the results of our work and say, 'I did this,' it diminishes everything we do here. I should not need to remind anyone that this is not a matter of you and your personal power.

"This circle will exist as long as you are all living. When one passes on, the Council is dissolved and you will go your ways as destined. I am from a previous council, and I bring continuity and the greetings of a great lineage."

I suddenly sensed extreme age in him, despite his prime-of-life appearance.

"As long as humans have lived on Earth, there has been a Council. It is possible that one or all of you will serve in my role after this one is dissolved. It is also possible that some of you will meet each other in daily life. Some of you are conscious of your presence here. Others are here in their dreaming. It does not matter. Some of you also have specific duties beyond those we all currently share. The scribe here, for example," he said, turning suddenly in my direction. "It has been determined that some of this work should be known.

"Now we begin. As long as humans have walked here, Earth has been in what might be called crisis. What happens when we are gone? All I can say is that part of our work is to sustain her. But at this point, she is in even greater crisis. Greater action is called for. She *will* be saved, if you want to put it that way, but it will be because of your work. Such is the nature of time and destiny." He smiled but then frowned slightly. "You will find this responsibility a joy and a burden." And then he was silent, gazing into the fire.

We looked inward, considering everything he had told us.

"Let us join hands," he said, lifting his gaze abruptly. "Just feel the energy. Feel the hands in yours."

We did so and focused on the sensation. I was familiar with this from working with archetypal energies, forming circles of hands in the inner world for harmonizing, and could feel our combined energy gathering, coalescing, and then flowing. Unlike archetype work, this felt warmer, human, material. And unlike the archetypes it seemed more unformed, potential rather than cool and focused, fire more than electricity.

After a bit, we broke the circle. Arrow continued. "We will form a vision circle to help manifest a different future; dream it into existence. What would that future look like?"

The cork was out of the bottle. Everyone spoke at once. I remember the African woman saying forcefully, "A world in which no child lives in fear." I said, "A reconnection with Spirit. A world in which our leaders consider the effect their choices will have on seven generations to come. A world in which the water is fit to drink." I'm sure I went on.

"How can we arrive at this?" Arrow finally asked above the voices.

We considered. Where to start? The longer we looked, the more it seemed that most of the turmoil and struggle affecting the Earth began with us. Arrow led us deeper.

"The proper relation of humans to the Earth is reciprocity. We hold her in honor and express our gratitude. She sustains us. When that is forgotten, things begin to fall apart ever so slowly. In the end, the Earth does not react to the ungrateful plundering but to the accumulation of heavy thought forms humans are so good at creating. It is an old cycle. At this first meeting, we will begin simply. Join hands and understand to your core that reciprocity is the ground on which all our work is based."

As we did so, I saw how this purest and most ancient of heart songs energizes anything that draws upon it. It was a deep lesson.

"Now consider the Earth as a planet. Step away and what do you see?"

Still holding hands, we saw our beautiful home shrouded in layers of dark, greasy fog. Space, on the other hand, was filled with living light, and the nearby planets were singing with joy. The shifting fog prevented most of that light from penetrating.

"This is the accretion of centuries of unenlightened thought and action, which organized religion has played a large part in sustaining," said Arrow. "Our work tonight is simply to visualize starlight sifting through that black mist into the Earth and all human hearts."

We focused on the image until Arrow finally broke the circle.

"Enough!" And the energy subsided. "Now you also realize that your work will continue each day with these images. This is your homework," he said grinning and leaning forward. "We meet again at the next new moon!"

With that the Council broke. Several people departed immediately. Others lingered, mostly in silence, enjoying the fire and each other's company.

I asked a question. "What is the orientation of this cave?"

Arrow laughed, "You can tell that."

True, I was being lazy. I opened to it and felt that north was about between Paqo and the African lady, which meant I was sort of in the south and the cave entrance was somewhat northwest.

"That's about right," said Arrow. I found it interesting that the cardinal directions didn't seem very significant here. What seemed more important was the crystal in the alcove behind Arrow. It wasn't a separate piece, as I had thought earlier. Rather, the entire mountain was a crystal, or at least it was crystal on the interior.

Arrow smiled. "An ancient place, used continuously for many thousands of years. It serves to amplify our efforts."

It was time to go. Almost an hour had passed and my physical legs were cramping from sitting cross-legged. I stepped into the space outside the cave and hung there. Several others were also there, moving slightly up and down. It was cool but not cold. Summer. South America, then, for I was sure the journeying took place entirely in the Middle World. I looked down valley to the southwest and could see scattered lights in the far distance. The sight was unexpected but somehow comforting. While the people there might not know of our presence or the cave, it reminded me of our human connection.

Red Feather had sat quietly behind me without joining hands, though he was aware of everything, including my thoughts. It must have been overwhelming. We journeyed back the way we had come. I opened my eyes in my room and heard him say only, "Very powerful."

Next morning I sought to discuss the event with my guide, Amun. He had little to say about it other than to urge me to accept it without reservation. It was a Monday, and I was depressed most of the day. That surprised me. Perhaps it was a realization of the burden Arrow had mentioned, or possibly that my career and the work I enjoyed doing well suddenly had less meaning.

3

The Traveler Returns

Twelve days later, Aquila announced, "He's here." But I already knew the Traveler was back.

I went to meet him, not sure I appreciated his coming and going in my inner world. We spoke. He told me that he would be helping me to connect with people and groups now living on Earth engaged in shamanic work. I had other things I wanted to do that day and left him, uneasy about the whole thing. A one-time appearance felt like an affirmation. A repeat visit felt more like invasion. Nor did he leave. During my daily routines over the next several days I could feel him waiting, when I thought about it. I put the meeting off.

A few days later, feeling strangely depressed again, I had a strong urge to see my guide, Amun. I could meet the Traveler on the way, if I chose.

Aquila just said, "He still waits," and then turned his head away to indicate disapproval. Maybe he didn't like the Traveler's hat.

We approached him at the same place, the head of the valley beneath the protecting mountain. As before, he wore skins from head to toe. He had a tiny fire going but rose as we emerged from the brush, unperturbed that I had made him wait. The moment now felt right.

"I will never enter farther than this," he said, looking forcefully into my eyes. I felt the connection and noticed that unlike my guide I could see all of him at once, not just an aspect. "Let us travel," he said.

Before I could agree, we were skimming a vast boreal forest in deep night and deep cold. There were no lights other than stars. Then there was a small cabin below us with a bit of smoke curling from a hole in the roof. Entering through the smoke hole, we saw a young woman lying on a low bed, dressed in red- and white-decorated animal skins. A shaman hovered over her, and two older women dressed in similar fashion sat against a wall. Embers smoldered in a fire pit in the center of the room. The shaman, a short, thick man, nodded toward us, sensing more than seeing, more relieved than surprised. He had a small rattle in his hand. I glanced at the woman on the bed. Her eyes were closed and there was sweat on her forehead. The shaman stepped back, fatigued. Looking more closely at the woman I saw a nasty form moving within her lower abdomen so strongly that at times it actually pushed the skin out slightly but horribly. He had only managed to provoke it. I turned to the Traveler.

"She needs your help," he stated without moving his eyes from the scene.

"Why me?"

"It's one of your specialties." He smiled slightly, perhaps knowing that I had asked for an affirmation of my path the previous day. Nodding toward the shaman he continued seriously, "He has done all he can do and has asked for our help. We're just in time."

I considered how I might approach this and decided to do it exactly as I had learned it, though later I was able to rely more on intent than tools. All my ceremonial objects were in a different room from where I was meditating. I didn't want to break focus so simply visualized them in hand as I had done in waking life on occasion. A big, double-pointed crystal appeared in my right hand. I placed it in the woman's left hand, still holding it loosely.

As soon as I began to extend my vision within her, I saw a powerful, angry ghost. I thought for an instant that it might be sorcery or something from a past life but quickly saw that it had simply seized the opportunity when a somewhat heedless and defenseless young woman came along. I kept seeing a place like a small stone quarry, but it meant little to me. Of course as soon as I touched the entity, it also saw me.

"What can you do that he hasn't already tried?" it sneered.

It was male, like oily smoke, but so dark that no light penetrated it. He became a spitting snake, wrapping a thick tail around her low spine and moving his head wildly.

"She is mine."

I knew not to waste time in such cases engaging in dialogue or returning fear for fear or hate for hate. On one of my journeys to the Lower World, an infinite garden whose mighty lord I know well, I received a conch shell horn to be used on occasion of need to summon an army of helpers. Such a shell came into my life soon thereafter. I now visualized that shell in my left hand and sounded the call. The army poured forth, leveling spears, lances, and fire at the intruder. Then they began their slow march out of the bowels, up through the chest, and into the left shoulder.

At times it seemed the soldiers—I always thought of their number as 80,000 for some reason—lost focus slightly and had to take a few steps back to regroup, but they never lost control of the situation. At the same time I became aware of the entity's name and used it as a command. We continued down the left arm, the entity writhing and twisting in anger and fear, but he could not find a way past the golden spear points. Suddenly he saw the crystal pulsing with soft clear light and moved into it. At that point I snatched the crystal away, being careful not to let either end point in someone's direction, particularly my own. I had learned the hard way about that. Instead I visualized it sealed temporarily in a pouch.

The atmosphere in the room lightened. The shaman nodded in thanks without looking up, and the two older women shifted. The young woman opened her eyes, smiled with relief, and then went into sleep. I removed handfuls of dense matter from her second-lowest energy center and then illuminated it with the light of Spirit. When I was satisfied, I looked at the Traveler. He motioned with his chin. Holding the pouch with the crystal, I passed with him through the door.

Outside, dawn approached. The air was extremely cold and still. I visualized a small, hot fire and opened sacred space within the six directions. Then as the slightest edge of the sun became visible I went about the business of releasing the entity into a place of refuge. I had considered leaving the job for later with the physical crystal but decided it was too volatile to have in the vicinity of my house.

One thing I noticed during this episode was how much easier it had been to do the work in a disembodied state. At the time, I relied more on sensing than seeing, but as I removed the crystal from its bag I could see the entity within it. I could also feel the general power of emotions and intent. Keeping compassion in my heart, I moved the crystal through the fire and then in one motion blew the entity out through the larger end toward the south. I could actually see the heaviest part shoot off. With each direction, moving clockwise, I could see finer and finer aspects departing the crystal until after the East nothing was left. I was impressed and gratified to actually see what I had only understood until then.

We remained for a moment, then the Traveler nodded and we flew off. I believe he accompanied me almost back to my world. Aquila was where I had left him. That part of the meditation had lasted about thirty minutes, but the work seemed like several hours.

When I met Amun, his eyes crinkled at the corners slightly, then he remarked, "How about that?"

4

Rain

-February-
New Moon in Pisces

I was at a workshop on the southern California coast. Coming from my wintry mountain home, I anticipated some warmth and the opportunity to shed a few layers of clothing. Instead, it rained a cold sea rain on the second day, intensifying with evening. Our session ran well into the night. At the end I was too tired to join the Council on the exact time of the new moon. My accommodation was a wood-floored tent with a four-poster bed, and I fell asleep to the sound of a monsoon-strength downpour on the canvas.

The next morning I awoke in the cold before dawn knowing that the sky had cleared. I arose and journeyed to the Crystal Cave with Red Feather. It was daytime there, but the interior of the cave was dark, lit only by the small fire before Arrow.

"Welcome!" he said exuberantly. "We have been awaiting you…two," and he looked slightly to my left. Red Feather and I took our seats. Without my asking, he answered, "You all take this as a sacred responsibility. None of you will miss a gathering except for once, and that has been foreseen."

A wave of absolute trust washed over me. Looking around, I could see everyone else experiencing the same feeling.

"You have done well," he continued. "In the time since we last met, all of you have kept that image, the image of golden universal energy piercing and burning away the dark fog surrounding Earth. It has energized everything. Can you feel it? Now it is time to cool things down a little. There is another energy, a ray, blue-green. It is love, but cooler, calmer. Picture our Earth in that beam, surrounded by it, informed by it. Picture that love informing the hearts of all humans, cooling their inflamed thoughts. Let it descend on those who are open. Do not force!"

We linked hands. I found it hard to focus because a big truck had rattled up and was idling outside my tent. I heard two men talking. They needed to erect a large pavilion for another group and were sizing up the space. I heard one say to the other, "How big? Well that ain't gonna fit." I laughed, knowing the back story, but it broke my concentration.

Without looking at me, Arrow said, "We all have demands on our attention."

I saw a picture of one of the female Council members doing her best to maintain concentration in the back room of a small adobe house. In the front, separated only by a curtain, there was domestic pandemonium.

I redoubled my focus, seeing the light bathing the Earth change from blue-green to turquoise. After a while we stopped. It was certainly easier to hold an image and channel energy with twelve others, but even so it was demanding.

"Now we will focus on something more specific." Arrow said. "The Earth, our Mother, has held off as long as she could, but it is time for her changes. It is not punishment, nor is it because of something humans have done. It is just time. You must put into open hearts that they should not fear."

I saw tectonic movements beginning along the coast of South America as far north as Mexico, destruction, fear, and perplexity. "How can we do this?" I wondered to myself.

"Make it rain," Arrow said aloud. "Send a drop into each open heart informing it that this is not retribution. It is a time of joy. Death itself is only a transition — if it comes to that."

We linked and created a vision of a fine mist of blue-green droplets descending into human hearts. Many hearts were closed, but there were enough that we felt a palpable lightening of spirit — even amid devastation in some places.

Suddenly it was time to end. An hour had passed and just beyond my tent the process of measuring, head shaking, and unloading the pavilion was well underway. I wondered again about recording everything.

Arrow said, without looking at me, "Because it should be known, Scribe."

I moved into the air outside the cave mouth.

The tall African man was already there, scanning the distance. His face was thin but strong, and he wore a robe in mustard- and black-printed cloth with a matching cap. He turned to me and said warmly, "We have a connection. I look forward to the day we meet in the flesh."

I knew the truth of his words.

"So do I."

5

Release

~March~
Full Moon in Virgo

Only two weeks had passed, yet I felt the Traveler's presence again. I told myself I was busy and had many things demanding my attention in both inner and outer worlds. Aquila just looked at me. I knew I would need to meet him of course. Still, the idea of someone camping, literally, in my inner world, as well as the ease with which he was able to do so, continued to bother me. "Let him wait," I thought petulantly.

A few mornings later, I finally approached him in the place that now seemed to be his. Wet spring snow was falling. Unlike some people's inner worlds or gardens—at least what I have heard—certain parts of mine are ever shifting. This place, a hanging valley surrounded by mountains with a volcano in the distance changed daily and seasonally in accordance with normal earthly cycles. Its weather often presaged something similar in the outer world by a day or two. I had also found an actual geography to these inner domains. A right turn here or a left turn there put me in front of doors or portals of various types—most of them nondescript or unlike doors at all. They led to different places. A systematic exploration would have been the work of a lifetime, however, and there were always more immediate issues—such as finding out what the Traveler wanted.

He had a small fire going in spite of the soaking snow. Without surprise he stood to greet me.

"You are needed."

"I will return at the end of my day."

"Good, but do not delay much longer."

I went about my very important business, but even in the outer world I could feel him patient at his small fire. That evening I returned with Red Feather.

"Welcome to you both," said the Traveler. "Let us journey."

We rose quickly out of the valley into a brief space of pure black and then we were above a city that looked eastern European. A pale winter sun shone. I could see dark tile roofs, punctuated in the near distance by a tall church spire. Farther off there seemed to be a river. Then we were in a room in the upper story of a house. It was sparsely furnished with a chair, a dresser, and a bed. The floor was clean and bare. Sunlight came through the windows. Everything seemed white. A young mother sat by a bed piled with pillows and a deep comforter. There, a girl of about eight lay dying, desiring release yet stuck. Two smaller children were in the room, a boy and a girl, and several spirit figures stood quietly in the corners.

"They have been waiting for you," said the Traveler. "The mother has prayed for help."

As soon as he spoke, she seemed to sense our presence and quietly removed the two children from the room, closing the door. The bedridden girl looked right at us and smiled. I turned to the Traveler with the obvious question.

"This is something you can do and from which you can learn. Your gift to her is also a gift for you."

I had never done a release for someone already dead, let alone dying, but his words gave me confidence.

"Begin," he said, moving back. "This is not my work."

I moved to the girl's head. Touching her dark blonde hair, I said, "Do not fear. It is time to pass over." She looked at me with wide but trusting eyes. Then I moved to her heart center and began the great unwinding, heart to solar plexus, heart to solar plexus to throat, counterclockwise in each energy center, counter-clockwise from center to center, finishing at the crown. I could see the light emanating from each center in little whirlpools, a different color for each.

It was obvious that she was dying from a degenerative nerve or muscle disease for which nothing more could be done. Her legs were already withered, and the lowest two centers were clogged with dark matter. I sensed that this was more related to the physical than the astral bodies. As I released the lower chakras, the dark matter came up and dissipated. She sighed in relief, for she had been living in a great deal of pain. I also learned some of her story. She was there to bring joy and comfort to her mother. Far from being a burden, she was a gladness in her mother's heart. The spirit-logic of apparent suffering and untimely death can be hard to understand. I only knew that her time was at an end and that my job was to facilitate her passing.

About the time I released her third-eye chakra, I sensed she was ready to go, but I continued my work until all the seven primary energy centers were released. Red Feather was opposite me watching.

"Help me lift her spirit," I said.

He hesitated. Without a physical body of his own, no doubt the energetics of the situation were much stronger for him.

"Go on," I urged. "You will be safe."

We reached under and into the girl's body, even though her luminous form was already rising. We lifted it straight up and she was out. Suddenly a great, luminous aperture opened exactly like a camera lens. A living, golden light shone from it and a figure stood just inside. Farther back I could see other figures waving and beckoning as if on a cruise ship, urging her to join. The closest figure simply stood there but emanated a steady presence of love and joy. The entire room filled with golden light, drowning the winter sun. The girl's luminous body moved toward the portal. She stopped to kiss her mother and then passed quickly into the golden passage toward the figures. The being at the entrance looked at us, nodded, and then the portal closed in on itself and was gone. In the silence, I realized that there had been a rushing noise. After a few moments, I sealed each of the chakras on the body and stood aside.

There was a still, emptiness in the room, broken only by the mother's quiet weeping. I understood then that her grief had restrained the girl's passage. I could also sense the girl's desire that her life and passing be celebrated, not mourned. Whispering in the mother's ear, I suggested that she light a candle to honor her daughter's undying flame, now released from pain. She brightened, stood up, and opened the door.

The two children entered, fully aware of the situation. The eyes of the younger one, a girl of about three, widened and she asked, "Mama, who are all these people?"

Her mother smiled. "Friends."

I noticed that the sun was setting. Had it been that long? I knew that if it was indeed somewhere in eastern Europe then the time difference would have been seven or eight hours at the most between where I was sitting and where this occurred. If anything, it should have been dawn in the room.

The Traveler looked amused. "It did take all afternoon, before you sat down in your own room. Now we must leave."

With Red Feather we shot straight into space and starlight. I could feel the light bathing us, washing away whatever wasn't ours.

"I will take you where you can find a way to our meeting place, but I will not go there myself," the Traveler said.

Soon, Red Feather and I were back at the campsite. I looked up across the valley to see Amun raise an arm, and then we were in the room where we started. Red Feather seemed fatigued. I was quietly pleased but also experiencing a slight bit of doubt.

What had happened?

6

Eclipse

~March~
New Moon in Aries

The exact time of the next new moon was unclear to me, but I held one night open. It seemed appropriate because the preceding day there was also a full solar eclipse, visible across much of the globe. In the early evening I heard Arrow say very plainly, "We are waiting."

Red Feather and I went to the edge of my valley and then to the Crystal Cave. It was night, and the stars were sharp in the moonless dark. Far in the distance I could see the cold electric lights of the town, but the glow from the mouth of the cave, high in its sheer rock face, was warm and inviting. I wondered whether it was visible to someone who might have made the intense physical effort to scramble over the sharp rocks that filled the canyon floor.

We entered. I expected someone to say, "Well, finally," but there were only welcoming nods. Nobody seemed in any hurry. In fact we weren't even the last. From my place, I looked around and realized that Alfred was still on his way. It gave me a chance to fix the other members again in my memory. The woman on Arrow's right remained a mystery to me. Previously, I thought that I might know her in daily life, but now I was certain I didn't. Nor did she seem like the others. Whereas I sensed a certain good humor from most, I felt something more hard edged and impatient in her. Perhaps we needed that energy to keep things focused.

When Alfred arrived, Arrow gave him a chance to settle in and then said calmly, "Let us begin. Link hands and focus again on the image of our Earth, our Mother, bathed in a soft, golden light. Give her your love."

We sank into the warmth. I could feel the simple strength of our purpose.

When we broke the link, I noted that Arrow seemed quieter than in the earlier gatherings. He stared into the fire.

"What is the most basic and direct thing we can do?" he asked finally.

Several people began to speak at once.

"Each will speak in turn. You begin," Arrow said, turning slightly in my direction.

I hesitated and then voiced what I had been thinking. "In the past month I have come to understand that we must help Earth give birth to herself, hold space for her."

The small woman on my left said, "People must not fear, they must know they are immortal and connected to Spirit."

Next to her, the Chinese fellow said, "Balance must be restored, male and female, light and dark."

Others carried on. After each spoke I thought to myself, "I wish I had said that!"

How could I hope to remember all that was said? We were suddenly in council, and this was almost like trying to memorize minutes.

The Amazonian shaman said, "We have seen how things in their current course will end and are deeply concerned. We must find a different thread."

Alice said, "We must restore health on all levels at once, from the microscopic to the planetary. It is all the same."

Paqo said, "Bring our relation with Pachamama back into balance and harmony. Ask her what she needs."

The African woman said, "Restore the feminine to a place of respect. All this war and violence makes her head hurt."

And so on around the circle.

Finally, the woman on Arrow's right spoke sharply, "Love, not fear."

Arrow nodded. "Each of these is equally important, but your words are the basis for everything," he said, turning toward her.

I asked a question. "You said we will manifest a different future, dream it into existence. How are we doing that?"

He considered for a moment and then addressed the group.

"The outcome is certain. How we get there is a matter for us. Today the great eclipse marks a point of changes for our Mother that will continue until the next eclipse several years hence. Let us join hands again and open to her voice."

I soon realized that our living Mother Earth was not simply spinning along in her path aware of her own destiny and how it was going to unfold. Instead she was slightly confused, knowing that she had to make a leap in her own spiritual evolution but hesitant, balancing on the edge of the unknown. I also saw how much those human thought forms grounded in fear kept her from making the next step. It reminded me somewhat of my last experience with the Traveler when I saw the effect of the mother's grief on her newly deceased daughter's ability to transition. As Earth hesitated, human fear fed on itself, making the inevitable worse. But part of the Earth's hesitation was out of love. I was surprised. I believe the others saw the same. Then I saw the Earth changes: volcanoes, earthquakes, tidal waves, and rising sea levels.

Arrow broke the circle. "Understand that none of this is punishment! It is important to let this knowledge inform your thoughts and actions. You will all be islands of strength in the time soon to come. This kernel, this seed, will give many around you comfort and will help counter the tide of fear. From you it will be planted in many other hearts. You see now that our own fear is causing harm and creating its own momentum. But remember that your work in our two meetings and in the interim has laid the basis for her to make her step. Link again. Give her your love once more, but this time bathe her in golden light. Communicate from your hearts that there is nothing to fear. Hold her in your thoughts as you would hold a newborn."

As we did so, I could feel a sense of relaxation and then her joy as she took a step into her becoming. We released hands after awhile. Many were smiling to themselves.

"And now the last piece for the night," continued Arrow relentlessly. "To dream a new future, we must begin with human hearts. Picture a rain like last time, but this time it is different: golden drops turning into crystals of insight and understanding, one for each heart on Earth. Remember that there is no coercion in matters of the spirit. Do not force."

I saw the African man nodding his head and realized that in daily life he might be called a Muslim, for a well-known Qur'an verse states the same.

"We will also do it a little differently. Each of you journey in thought to the places you see fit. The entire globe must receive this rain."

I thought for an instant about a journey within a journey, but then we joined hands and were off.

Naturally most people went to their homelands first. I found myself in North America and was aware of several others. And then I was in the Middle East, following the great swath of the day's eclipse, Kabul, Baghdad, Cairo, North Africa. I pulled great drops of molten gold from the light surrounding the Earth and watched as they changed into crystals and watered parched hearts. Many crystal drops were willfully rejected or simply bounced off hearts that had shells like walnuts. Some hearts were too withered to accept anything at all. But more of the rain seemed to find a welcome than before. As I moved across North Africa, I saw my African friend coming up from the south.

"Africa is a lot of work," he said with a slight laugh.

We crossed into Europe and separated. Someone had already been there and left little for us to do. I moved through Russia and then into East Asia, sensing that someone had already been in the south. I even hit Antarctica briefly for the few people living there and then moved up to South America. It too seemed well covered. Suddenly we were back in the cave.

"Excellent work!" said Arrow. "Now we are done."

It had been a long night. At first nobody left, quietly sitting to gather a little energy for the trip back to daily life while considering what we had done. I had not noticed before but now I saw that the fire in front of Arrow wasn't a wood fire at all but more like an alcohol fire. It seemed to be burning nothing other than air.

As if in response, Arrow said, "Time for a little cleansing."

The fire roared up to the ceiling entirely in shades of green. I suppose there was heat but what I most noticed was how good it made me feel. After a while it dropped down. People began to leave, but I stayed on a little longer.

"I am concerned that I will not be able to remember everything that happened tonight," I said to Arrow.

"Do not worry," he replied. "You will do the best you can, and you have plenty of help. By the way, this book you're experiencing will have thirty-six chapters."

I assumed he meant there would be thirty-six Council meetings but immediately remembered that other episodes were also finding their way into the text.

Red Feather and I stood to leave. I had forgotten my friend though he was fully present.

Arrow looked up at me. "How many more signs do you need?" he asked, referring to my pending decision to leave my career and walk the medicine path.

On the drive back from California right after the previous Council meeting, I decided make a leap I thought might come one day but had certainly not been actively seeking. Suddenly it was right, but then I was unable to get a meeting with my boss. Her office was in a different building, ten minutes' walk away. The days slipped by, while I told myself that I needed to tell her at the right time. Our regular meetings suddenly seemed pre-empted by her travel schedule and committee work.

"Visualize it!" Arrow said with a touch of exasperation. "But not here!"

We moved out into the night. I was suddenly filled with a simple desire to fly and zoomed toward the town lights. As I approached I could see it was a dusty mining enclave, not even a town, really. Some distance farther, the sea crashed against endless miles of empty shore. The settlement was asleep except for a cantina holding a few people intent on their drinking.

We continued out over the ocean and then dived in. There were orcas. They were only a little surprised to see me. How often did such things occur? From them I learned that until recently these had been prime hunting grounds for seal, but in the last several seasons the take had thinned. In return I told them what I was doing in the neighborhood. Mostly we played. And then with Red Feather I shot into the air, bee-lined back to our starting place, and moved up through the Earth to the room in which I was sitting.

An hour had passed. I was tired and Red Feather seemed faint, as if there was less of him there. I went right to bed. Another heavy rain was falling.

7

A Curse

Now Aquila told me there were more intruders. He disliked these events and remained distrustful of the Traveler. This time it wasn't even the Traveler. Aquila led me to the lower end of the hanging valley and an overlook high above the river plain below. We gazed down on its braided, shallow stream. I had been down there a few times to explore but not recently. The water seemed to run through tundra and even in summer was always frigid and clouded with glacial milk.

It was daytime, mid-spring. The winter snow and ice were in full melt. Where the water was visible it ran high. On a far bank, we could see a group of seven or eight men moving carefully down the plain. At a certain point the one who seemed to be the leader looked up in our direction, sensing something. We remained hidden and watched them pick their way into the distance. They appeared unaccustomed to this sort of thing, but I was uneasy. Parts of my inner world were more like a hotel lobby lately.

A few days later, Aquila said, "They are camped at the far end."

It seemed they were waiting for something. We went to investigate. As we came off the high, ground, I suddenly decided not to present myself in human form — if it came to that — and assumed the wolf-shape I used when Aquila and I hunted in this realm. The leader of the party would know I was human, but I was already feeling slightly invaded and didn't want to just throw the door open.

It was early evening. We approached their small fire cautiously and sat beyond the ring of light to observe. They were in a half-circle, open in our direction. Most of the group seemed to be drowsy or asleep, but the leader soon felt our presence and looked right toward us.

I approached while Aquila remained out of sight. The man was relatively short, slightly stocky, and was dressed in animal skin with the hide on the outside. He had a spear—the only weapon in the whole group. What struck me most were his blue eyes. "Sámi," I thought to myself—Laplanders.

"What do you seek?" I asked.

If he was surprised to meet a talking wolf, he didn't show it. Rather, he seemed relieved. "We seek help," he replied. "These men have expended great energy assisting me to journey. I do not know where I am, but I feel we are here because you can do something for us." He waited for a reply, but I said nothing.

"There is a curse on our village," he finally continued. "We are withering."

I did not sense deceit and accepted his words. As I noted earlier, it does not seem possible to tell a lie in a place where the energetics are essentially naked.

"I must consider this," I said, and moved back into the shadows.

The next day I returned as a human.

Time, as we commonly experience it, is variable there. In this part of the inner world are day and night, seasons and weather. Nevertheless, consecutive visits can happen all in the same night or day or skip days at a time. The key to remaining alert and receptive lies in avoiding anticipation or presupposition. Everything conveys information. Now, although a day had passed in my outer world, I knew it was the same night in the inner world. The leader sensed my coming, although none of his fatigued friends even looked up.

"I will try to help you," I told him. "I do not know how, but because you are here there must be a reason. It will be sometime in the next three days," by which I meant outer-world time. "How will I find you?"

He considered. "I will leave this green stone. Return here and use it to reach our village."

When I journeyed the next morning, I could tell the Sámi were gone. I wanted to ask Amun about it.

"They need you. Use caution," was the sum of his reply.

I returned that evening, having carefully opened sacred space between the six directions, opened my medicine bundle, dressed in black, and prepared some tools—the usual precautions. Red Feather also agreed to come. All day I could feel his slight anxiety. In some ways the risk was greater for him.

Before I met Aquila, I also asked my protector to join us. He, or it, was a large black shadow, shaped like one of those blocky rock-art figures one finds in the American southwest and elsewhere. His presence was more like an absence, the absence of any light. Like many of those one encounters in this particular part of the inner world, he was able to navigate it as well as the outer world. I will tell more of him and his nation soon, for some of this story includes them.

So there were four of us.

Aquila seemed determined to chaperone the outing and told me to assume wolf form again. Looking at Red Feather, more visible in this setting, he said, "You could be a flicker, but it might attract attention. They don't fly at night."

"I will be a raven," Red Feather said. "They're black."

It was hard to tell whether Aquila appreciated my friend's brand of humor. And were ravens any more nocturnal?

As we prepared, I happened to look up to the place I normally met Amun. A tiny light twinkled. Red Feather noted it as well.

"You know, your guide is also among the great ones," he said.

It was a nice thought, but I couldn't dwell on it. We moved out quickly. Beginning our descent to the valley, I turned again toward Amun's place and saw another twinkle. It reminded me of something. In humility I called on Spirit for help and guidance and then set an intention that the outcome be for the highest good of all.

We reached the place the Sámi campsite. Their fire still smoldered. Aquila lifted his leg on it in annoyance, but I knew they had left it that way by design. The small green stone lay nearby in the packed snow. I took it up in my mouth. Instantly we were in a birch forest looking down into a village beneath a clear, moonless evening. The countryside was relatively flat, but the settlement sat in a slight bowl. It consisted of ten or twelve log cabins and tarpaper shacks plus a few large tents. Smoke wisped here and there from chimneys. The months-long boreal night was over, and spring approached, although there was still plenty of snow. I saw no evidence of any ceremony or prayer circle underway, which was probably intentional.

It seemed best to sit and watch, for I was unsure how to proceed.

Slowly I discerned a dark cloud over the village, obvious once I stopped trying to find something. Aquila sniffed as a reminder to use my nose. He sometimes pointed out that I relied too much on sight alone. Now I smelled rot. I was aware that there were no children and that in a few of the dwellings people were stone drunk. There was a reindeer corral nearby filled with a number of scrawny animals. Some seemed sick. I wondered what I could do, resisting the urge to panic. Nothing came to me.

We withdrew a small distance. It was unwise to linger too long, and I needed to widen the circle, find out more. The only strategy that came to mind was the one I sometimes use when fishing. Coming on a new stream it is tempting to throw a line right in and see what happens. Start doing something. Yet the better course is often to observe for a while, allow any startled fish to resume their stations, and see what they do. It would be easy enough to lift the immediate curse, but what about its creator? And what allowed the curse to take hold and flourish?

Opening my eyes in the darkened room where I sat in meditation, I took a tracking stone from my medicine bundle, then immediately changed to a more specialized stone for tracking open energetic wounds. That stone always went to blood. I scanned a widening radius around the village. Deeper in the birch forest, perhaps a mile off, I saw a horrible sight. Things were busy feeding on what appeared to be a dead reindeer, though it crossed my mind that the meal could also have been human. What were they? There were three, between four and five feet high, neither human nor animal, and not entirely physical. When they stood from their feeding they seemed stooped; their heads were covered in gore from thrusting inside the steaming body cavity. Wolf-men? No, something else. They were very alert, and it seemed best not to view them too long. I widened the circle farther.

A few leagues to the east a sorcerer sat in his own shack, staring into a small fire, muttering. I saw the story too, for he was stewing in it. Perhaps ten years before, he was ejected from the village for practicing his sorcery. He had spent much of his time since then reinforcing the curse he laid at the time. Now it was easy to follow the energetic lines to its creator. And he had also created or summoned those creatures to torment and terrify the village. Where he had learned that little trick?

He became aware of my tracking. Quietly I withdrew my attention and seized another stone from my medicine bundle—invisibility. I asked my protector to envelop all of us in shadow, and then we sat still without thinking a thought or acknowledging an emotion. The sorcerer's gaze touched the village, scanning. He knew the village well and that something was up. We remained silent until he finally relaxed his attention somewhat, still vigilant. Then we pulled back even farther into the woods. I still didn't know what to do. How do you heal everyone in a village? Kill the sorcerer? It seemed crude, and I recalled my intent at the outset: the highest good for all. The night grew old. We waited.

At one point Red Feather said, "The best defense against sorcery is a living connection to Spirit."

Indeed. The people had forgotten that connection and its potential strength. Instead they had believed in the sorcerer's power and their own powerlessness as things slowly went rotten.

At length, the village shaman came to us in his dreaming. It was the green stone. I still had it and placed it on the ground so he would recognize it.

"Please release us," he begged.

"I am unsure what to do."

"Cut the cords. We cannot."

He withdrew. It was a bold move on his part, but for me it was as good a place to start as any. I took an obsidian blade from my kit and made cutting motions on the edge of the medicine bundle. In the inner world I saw the blade cutting the thick, dark cords of energy that surrounded the settlement and that ran to the sorcerer. It was like cutting steel cable. As the tightly twisted strands frayed and broke they sprang apart, curling back with an audible sound. When the last was severed, there was a tangible lightening in the village. More remarkable was the effect on the sorcerer. I had been monitoring him with part of my attention, watchful for a reaction. Now I realized that his cords had bound him too. He sat back, looked up, and sighed with relief. He knew what had happened, perhaps aware of my efforts all along. There would be no immediate reaction.

Still, it seemed a good idea to move fast. For one thing, I had never maintained a guise other than my own in the inner world for very long. I didn't know how effective it was, but sustaining it took conscious energy. I lit a large, resinous piece of wood and circled it over the stones in my bundle, which now represented the village. It flared brightly, scenting the air and burning off the dark cloud. When the flame reached my hand I blew it out and wafted the sweet smoke into each heart, including the sorcerer. I then took a large crystal and rotated it counterclockwise above the village representation to draw out the words of the curse and whatever affinities they had latched onto. Perhaps there was blame enough for all, but I wasn't interested in the stories and the old wounds. Time to make newer, brighter stories.

Lastly, I tracked the creatures of the sorcerer, now just moving off their feeding, and drew them into the crystal as well, enclosing it carefully in its pouch. They too had become a great burden to their creator, if he still had any control of them.

That was all I could do. We waited. Dawn approached, and people began to stir. One by one they stepped outside and opened their hearts to the sun and to Source, rediscovering their own strength. Most seemed unaware of each other. Even the sorcerer stepped into the sunlight and allowed it to enter his dusty heart. It was now up to the village shaman to sustain the renewed connection.

Leaving the green stone in a small clearing near the village, we set our intent to return, trying to leave no signatures by which we could be followed in the inner or outer worlds.

An hour and a half had passed, according to my clock. I was tired.

8

The Two Trees

-April-
New Moon in Taurus

I encountered nothing further after the work at the village, nor did Amun mention it.

At the new moon, six days later, I was in Puerto Rico for an academic conference. Although I had finally announced my plan to leave publishing for the shining reality of shamanic practice and to respond to the call of Spirit, my last day was still months off. Pride and attachment demanded that I leave matters as well in hand as possible. Part of me was already out the door, yet twenty-some years in the business, fifteen of them building and sustaining my own operation, were hard to walk away from. Everything I dreamed and set into motion much earlier had come to fruition, beautifully, though not without effort. It had been a fulfilling career, but I no longer had a sustaining vision. The new goal was hard to define and even harder to express to others, though I had no doubts about the path. In fact it had chosen me.

At this meeting, what used to energize me now felt hollow. The effort of seeking new projects, meeting people who wanted to publish manuscripts, greeting authors, and taking book orders—knowing it was my last time but announcing it only selectively—left me drained. I planned to journey the night of the new moon and declined a few dinner invitations. Yet I put off the work of the evening, dozing through the Spanish-language TV news and then more TV.

Suddenly it was time.

Red Feather and I journeyed to the crystal mountain. It was night. The cave mouth glowed from the fire within. I was always relieved when we weren't the last. Taking our place, I began to move my eyes clockwise around the circle, making contact with every person in turn.

Each returned my gaze, withholding nothing. In some I could even see a few past lives, though I did not linger very long. As I reached Paqo, the African woman arrived and took her place. I met her eyes and continued around to the woman on Arrow's right. I was even more certain I did not know her, yet I did. She smiled slightly. Arrow swiveled to meet my gaze too but only briefly.

"Let us join hands," he said, staring at the green fire burning before him about an inch above the floor. "Sense each other's energy, then sense the whole."

I could feel the different flavors and then felt the rising current.

"Now I will increase it."

Immediately the cool, electric flow grew stronger.

"Do not resist. Allow," he said.

His strong hand gripped mine. In my left I held the small, warm hand of the woman beside me.

"More," said Arrow, and the flow increased. He did this three more times, letting us grow used to the jump in current and cautioning us not to resist the flow. The final level was intense. I experienced it as a ring of living, white light moving through us all at great speed. Arrow soon broke the circle but I could feel it resonating, decreasing just a step or two.

"That is the low end of the levels at which we will soon be working," he said. "Your efforts have been good. You probably do not realize the effect you have had, but it has shifted things already. What shall we do now?"

There was silence. For my part I had simply expected that he would tell us what to do. Now it was suddenly our decision. To change the world, where does one start? I saw another dark, greasy cloud hanging over our planet—not as thick as before but still emanating from human ignorance. The ignorance was the darkness and fear resulting from disconnection from Spirit. It carried a sense of scarcity, vague hunger, and a feeling of deep separation. Yet the alienation itself was an illusion, though often actively sustained. We looked at each other. All had seen the same thing. Once again it seemed that Earth's problems came from human hearts.

We linked hands and without direction pictured a fine, golden mist enveloping the Earth. Arrow increased the amplitude to the previous highest level. The mist slowly settled to the surface and illuminated the hearts of good and ignorant alike with the love and certainty that comes from a living connection to Spirit. I felt the world pause. Then we each visualized the mist covering the globe again. In some places it seemed ready to fully dissolve centuries of accumulated darkness. Sitting physically on the floor of the hotel room, I felt it enter my own heart. We sustained the vision and the intent as long as we could and then released in unison.

After several minutes of reflection, people began raising their eyes. Arrow scanned the circle. "Someone tell a story!"

"I have one," the Amazonian said almost immediately. He looked down as if witnessing a vision and began.

"In my land there are two great trees, male and female. We believe they connect Heaven and Earth and in that way sustain the world. One day some white men came and asked permission and assistance in studying the plants of our forest. They said it would benefit all humankind, and we agreed. We told them some of what we know and even showed them the two trees. Later, without telling us, they bored into the heart of each tree and in so doing removed much of the spirit-force. We discovered this after they left. By then it was too late. The trees began to decline. Men and women no longer cooperated with each other or served one another. Instead they began to fight and bicker and made their lives miserable. That was the first sign. Worse followed." He fell silent.

"I think we should heal those trees," Arrow said after a moment.

We joined hands and followed our friend's thoughts to two immensely old trees standing about a quarter mile apart and rising well above the jungle canopy. They lived but were in bad shape. We went to the female first. A suppurating hole about chest high showed where the core sample had been removed. Directing our attention within, we could see there was still some flow of elements up and down her great trunk, but it was obvious that even this would not last much longer. She remained conscious but was deeply confused.

"Give her green light," Arrow directed.

We sent shades of green, healing energy up from the Earth and into the tree's system. The effect was immediate — at least to us — for we could follow it like time-lapse imagery: systems reviving, life extending into withering branches or seeking new outlets, leaves budding and unfurling. With that came all sorts of life, some that might be called parasitic but all of it now easily sustained.

We turned our attention to the male tree. He was nearly dead. Like many things male, it was outwardly stronger but inwardly more brittle.

"Red energy," said Arrow. "Careful!"

It seemed ineffective. The tree had already lost consciousness.

"Gold!" he said.

We saw, more than intended, gold energy coming from deep within the Earth, entering the root system, moving slowly up the diseased and infested channels to the withered crown and then back down into the Earth. As the circulation continued the tree regained consciousness and was gradually able to add life to the restarted systems much as the female had done. Green energy slowly mixed with the gold and then supplanted it. A great sense of relief suddenly filled our cave. Heaven and Earth were reconnected. We released our circle.

"Thank you," said our storyteller.

I shifted my eyes from him, wondering if someone else had a story, but that was enough work for the evening.

Arrow took some of the mystic fire. Handing it to me, he said, "Take some, put it in your body, pass it on."

It was neither hot nor cool, but it was certainly alive. I put some in my throat. Several others including Arrow placed it in their hearts; the Amazonian put it on top of his head; the European woman put it in her belly; the woman on Arrow's right swallowed hers. The cave filled with smiles.

People soon began to leave. I pushed back and leaned against the cave wall. It felt good.

"Scribe has a new toy," Arrow said, teasing, referring to my recently purchased but yet unused computer. "This will really help him write!" To all, he added, "Remember the gold mist and the two trees."

I looked past his back at the woman next to him. "Who are you?" I asked.

"You know me but not yet," she replied and smiled slightly. I sensed power.

Then it was our time to leave. The African man, Paqo, and I stood and walked into the air outside. I looked toward the tiny mercury-vapor lights of the sleeping town. Rather than go out to sea it felt better to shoot straight up. Where was this place? I wanted more perspective. The other two accompanied me. We saw a high coastal range extending in waves inland and stretching up and down the coast. Looking north, Paqo said, "South of my country."

"Nowhere near my country!" the African said.

We scanned the terrain a bit more, then Paqo shot off like a comet.

After a while the African said, "You must visit me. It will be good. Now I must go," and he too was gone.

9

Red Feather

To talk about Red Feather opens so many questions leading to further questions that I hesitate to do so at all. Neither he nor I know where our connection leads; yet we are both sure it is part of our individual destinies and is now a conscious choice for us both. He has become a trusted ally. More than that he is a beloved friend who walks with me in all worlds.

)

Early one autumn, several years prior to the primary events in this account, my wife and I spent time exploring some places in the Southwest. These were the ruins formerly inhabited by the ancestral Puebloans, those who are often called Anasazi. It was something we often did, though less so at this time due to our growing involvement in shamanic training and practice. Now returning to the sites where so many had lived over the centuries, we were intrigued to discover the near-audible echoes of those ancient voices. In some dwelling places, massive enough to house hundreds of people, we could tell the inhabitants had lived good lives full of happiness. Other places had dark echoes of war, brutality, and worse.

One in particular was so dark that we retreated in haste. Our hosts, people who knew the region much better than we did but who tended to dismiss the shamanic view, remarked disapprovingly that a local, contemporary Indian group had recently seen fit to destroy some of the ancient stone rooms there. I thought to myself that in fact they had exercised considerable restraint. Something conscious and dark pervaded the site. At yet another place I sensed very distinctly a watcher or guardian on the periphery and could almost make out a form in the long afternoon shadows.

Much of this was new to me. I was intrigued to find I could sense it so strongly whereas previously I would have blundered in, taken a

40

few photos, and looked to the standard archaeological explanations of population densities, resource utilization, and climatic shifts. Such approaches mostly treat the ubiquitous rock art as interesting but enigmatic decoration. We went home reflecting on the pleasant outing but quickly returned our attention to affairs of daily life.

In the next week my lower back began to ache. I attributed it to overexertion and thought it would pass eventually. Instead it became a constant companion. I initiated a course of visits to the massage therapist and the chiropractor, supplemented by extensive stretching and simple energy work. Nothing seemed to have any lasting effect, and I turned more and more to over-the-counter pain medication, taking much more than I ever had before. If someone had come to me with such an issue, I would have checked a few things immediately. But healers sometimes are their own worst patients. At the time, I did not have the wit or intuition to investigate other explanations and continued to assume it would just take a bit longer for things to improve. They didn't, and I became accustomed to the pain.

A chance for a shamanic session with one of my teachers arose at the end of November. At first I declined, but on reflection I thought it might be good to experience his work on an individual basis. In a few days I called to see if there was still an opening. There was. Besides, I realized I had a presenting issue.

When we met, I mentioned my growing suspicion around the timing of this affliction.

After some assessment, he said, "It is one thing to visit such places as a tourist. It's another to go as a shaman or seeker. People march into sites such as Machu Picchu and sit down to meditate, leaving themselves wide open. The spirits there will test them, maybe have a little fun. It gets trickier when one walks this path. You have something interesting I've only seen once before. It's a medicine man. You had your mesa with you. Correct? That, plus some of the other work you were doing attracted him to the lineage of medicine people you already carry. Right now he is living in a nightmare. He is digging two claws into your lower back just to hang on, though that's all of him actually in you."

He stopped to assess my reaction. I nodded for him to continue. It made sense.

"You have a choice. We can bring him into consciousness—he could

41

be a powerful ally — or we can remove him and send him to join his ancestors. If you decide to let him stay, I can't tell you how it will go."

"Let him stay." I knew immediately that I would have regretted the other choice for the rest of my life, though this one seemed very dangerous. I myself had extracted numerous disembodied spirits that had taken up residence in unwitting clients. Sometimes these spirits were deceased relatives, afraid to cross over or bound by cords built over a lifetime. Often, it was something nastier — and more than one.

I suppose this might be called possession, but after a few such encounters done the hard way it began to seem just part of a day's work, hardly requiring the overwrought efforts one sees in Hollywood films or hears about in other settings. Hosts tended to experience such things as depression, slides into substance abuse, insomnia, and constant fatigue, all of which could go on for years. Yet I learned after a while that none of these entities or energies was "evil." In the end, even the ones that seemed foulest could be removed and sent into the Light, or the Dark, if I approached them with respect — and a great deal of care.

I have described some of this process already. The hard part for me was cleansing the big crystals, if I used them. Until I learned to treat them like loaded guns with hair triggers, I kept getting Uncle Fred or the bad priest in me. After about a day, I'd find myself feeling strange and out of sorts. I came to know the signs and later learned to clear them myself with the assistance of Red Feather and other spirit helpers. But much of this was still new to me then and possibly unsafe. Considering my teacher's offer, I wondered. How much energy would it drain?

"Okay," he said. "Decide which side he will walk on."

I was relieved to know that my guest would not actually be in me.

"My left." I was used to having Amun walk on the right, though more in the inner world, and didn't want to confuse things.

Perhaps he expected me to choose the right side. I had not told him of my inner-guide work and the whole world that lay just below the surface. What did he see? He hesitated and then began. I lay face up briefly and then rolled to my stomach to allow better access to my back. It ached. To someone unfamiliar with the methods, it would have seemed like sideshow stuff: some feather work, some floral water, "playing Indian," as a combative client once dismissed the work. But I could feel all of it, as well as the deep conversation my teacher was having with this spirit, bringing him into consciousness, explaining, negotiating, releasing. I could also feel the two cruel hooks retracting somewhat out of my spine.

"Can you see him?" he asked at one point.

"Yes, I can see his face now."

"Good."

Finally he said, "This man has bird magic. If you agree to teach him how to journey, he will teach you some of his knowledge."

"I agree."

We finished our session, which had taken about an hour.

"Keep me informed how it goes. We'll call him Two Claws," he added with a smile.

A less-skilled practitioner, like myself, might have gone ahead and simply done the extraction. To this day I am grateful for my teacher's seeing and skill. My path is richer for it. I believe the same is true for my friend.

)

At first it was very strange but also very interesting. As my companion returned to greater awareness he was forthcoming with basic information, perhaps relieved to step out of his nightmare. He didn't like the name Two Claws, preferring Red Feather. One of his names was something like He'takála, which he said meant "man from the north" and is what the Anasazi called him. Even now I do not know the name he was given at birth because he says it is not something one shares. He said he traveled a fair distance from a place of mountains and more cold and snow. At one point he had a wife, whom he cherished, but another group sacked his encampment and she was killed. After that there were too many reminders of their life together. He moved south, working as a healer and practicing his bird magic.

He had heard that the Anasazi were adept at using power and sought to learn more. He found that to be true and learned much but also that they were obsessed with sorcery. He did not know how he died or even if he died, or how he came to be where he was—whether he was held at one particular site by sorcery, chose to remain as a guardian, or was waiting for something interesting to come by.

He confirmed that he was attracted both by the lineage in the plant medicine I had been experimenting with and by the lineage stone I carried. Perhaps he mistook the lineage for me and was confused when he realized the actual situation.

But immediately after coming more into conscious relation with me, he stood aloof for some days assessing the situation. I would have done the same. I could feel him slightly to my left, about a half-step back. Two things eased his concerns somewhat. One was when I cut myself carelessly while shaving and was able to feed my lineage stone, a practice that is part of my tradition. The other was a journey I took right to the Great Threshold. One can pass over, but one might not be able to return—or want to return. That really impressed him. He said that what also caused him to follow me was his sense that I had bird magic too, if only latent. On the other hand he was horrified by what he saw in a woman during an arduous training session soon after the work with my teacher. The energetics must have looked pretty gruesome to him. Yet each day I could feel his claws easing a little more out of my spine, though not entirely.

He was different from my guide. Amun never offered an opinion or advice unless asked. Red Feather had opinions on a number of things and didn't mind sharing. Our technology did not impress him. He said we make a mistake when we see it as an end in itself, though he liked cars and loved the idea of indoor plumbing. I sensed a great thirst, as if he came from a very dry place. He considered television all lies and distraction, but he liked nature shows. He found writing an amazing tool, and seemed to see pictures as I read. At one point he declared, "What does not serve our Mother Earth, serves no purpose at all," but seemed willing to accept that I didn't quite live by such a high standard. It raised some doubts for me.

)

A week after the initiation of this arrangement, my wife and I attended a fire ceremony at the conclusion of the training. The person whose session Red Feather earlier witnessed accompanied us to the site at the edge of a frozen lake. It was a very cold December night. When I had worked on this woman, I encountered what I took to be some major sorcery connected to a past life, including a ceremonial blade lodged deep in her third chakra. I was a little unprepared for the heavy lifting, but protected myself the best I could with several layers of defense and invisibility before following the event back. I dealt with it to the best of my ability, and although I sensed formidable skill from the initiator I also felt I hadn't left any footprints. During the ride out to the lake the woman talked a great deal about her experience, for she saw a lot of it herself. Letting her do so was probably a mistake.

At the lake a big group of about sixty people was gathered, braving the deepening cold. After the ceremony everyone quickly departed, including the woman. My wife and I volunteered to stay with the fire, enjoying the bright stars. About a half hour on, we were watching the embers, exchanging small talk, when I felt a sudden sharp claw in my spine just above the sacrum.

"There is danger!" someone said very clearly.

I had my back to the lake and turned but saw nothing. A notion that I should act fluoresced within me; yet I felt curiously disconnected, as if a vital circuit were shut down. It didn't occur to me to call my protector or activate some basic defenses. What could happen? It had been a pleasant evening, and I was warm. I disregarded the warning but could not shake the feeling of exposure. Finally I moved over to my wife's side of the fire to face the lake, trying to seem natural.

She immediately stopped what she was saying and asked, "What's up?"

I told her what I had heard and was feeling.

"Now that you mention it," she said, "it does feel creepy. Let's leave."

Suddenly I wanted to bolt. We moved to the car as quickly as possible without running. I couldn't disregard the feeling of being stalked, and we got out as quickly as possible.

A quarter mile along, my wife said, "I slammed the seat belt in the door. Slow down so I can open it and put the belt on."

I was reluctant to do so, but another part of me said, "Don't go into panic." After that, it seemed like a long drive back, with a surprising amount of oncoming traffic for this remote road. I really couldn't tell what the danger had been. Human? The temperature was well below freezing. Perhaps it was blowback from undoing someone's careful sorcery. But I did know that the warning came from my new friend. Suddenly things seemed a little more "interesting."

Back in the warmth and light, my wife said she couldn't find one of her mittens. It might have fallen out when she opened the car door for the seat belt. The thought of her mitten still at the lake left me uneasy. We discussed it again the next day and agreed to return for it. For one thing, they were very good mittens. I could picture where it might be, but part of me was also saying, "Trap!" We did go back that day, in a blinding snowstorm, which I thought was helpful, but could not see the mitten on the road or at the fire site. We were both on edge, didn't get out of the car, and didn't say anything until well away.

I mulled the whole thing for a few days before I thought of asking Red Feather to show me what he had seen. What I saw was some kind of dark, backlit figure or creature slowly vectoring in on that woman and me by energetic signature rather than the fire or car lights. I also saw that because of my indecision, we narrowly missed being intercepted. I still cannot say what that would have meant.

)

During the next four nights I did not sleep well. I thought it was just from processing all the work I had been doing, plus the events at the lake, but then I realized I needed to have a conversation with Red Feather. He said he trusted the reason we were sharing a path, though he did not know exactly what that might be. I liked him and could sense integrity. He was glad to teach me his bird magic and started with some basics right then. In response I said I was not sure I knew what to offer him, but he said that I could teach him to journey and project his consciousness. It seemed a strange request, given that he was the disembodied one. Indeed, earlier I had offered to take him part way to meet my guide, though not all the way, but he said, "Don't leave me somewhere I can't find my way back."

A shaman with whom I later discussed Red Feather told me that a hallmark of Middle World spirits is their inability to travel to the Lower or Upper Worlds—at least without assistance. I have found this to be true for Red Feather.

Red Feather also told me he could see something ahead that I might be able to offer. He said he would always watch my back just as he had at the lake. I expressed concern that he be able to accept my power animals, guide, and the rest of the committee that seemed to follow me around. He replied that he would honor them all and that when it came time to part ways, it would be my task and honor to send him into the Light or wherever he chose to go.

In the years since, we have reaffirmed our basic agreement several times. Perhaps he is here in his dreaming. When or how we may part ways I do not know, though it will be lonely without him. Or perhaps some day we will taste Infinity together.

10

Red Feather's Soul Retrieval

Several weeks after my conversation with Red Feather regarding our arrangement and about a year before the Traveler came calling, I awoke with a terrible backache. I thought it might be delayed reaction to all the cartons of books I had been moving in my warehouse trying to keep up with the younger guys. Checking more closely I could tell that Red Feather had lost some consciousness and was digging in. I felt old and drained. We were both experiencing a disconnection from the lineage of shamans and healers. For him, it caused mild panic that threw him into his old mode.

I worked with the lineage stone that two of my teachers had gifted me. Holding it behind my back, I reassured him that the connection would always be there. Finally I conveyed that while I would never evict him, if we were to work together I could be more effective if I was not in pain and he wasn't drawing so much energy. I requested that he limit himself to two small threads for now and save the claws for warning. He said he understood and that he was sorry his fear caused me to suffer. Was it embarrassment I sensed? Almost immediately my pain eased. After several hours my back was much looser and my energy level was rising.

Things settled down after that. He was more conscious but somehow less immediate. At the same time, I felt his consciousness subtly informing mine, particularly when I was outside, away from the city, or even just looking at the sky while stopped in traffic. He always noted the birds, yet he was also slower to offer unsolicited opinions. That may have come from a greater familiarity with my life and an acceptance that much of our modern world is divorced from nature and Earth and that we just don't recognize many of the signs and signals that were so obvious to him.

Generally, I was aware of him as a presence on my left, though sometimes he came around to my front and we held our palms together for a stronger communication. I encouraged him to range a little more freely, but he seemed content. He never appeared in my dreams. It was also something new to realize that he was aware of my every thought.

Over several weeks I pondered whether it might be useful to do a particular type of soul retrieval for Red Feather. I posed the question to Amun.

"Why don't you ask him?"

I did, with some explanation. The concept seemed new to him, though he already knew my question. "I will think on it," he said. I expected an interval of days, if not weeks, but ten minutes later he returned as if from a distance with an emphatic yes. I didn't do it immediately, and for the next two days I sensed impatience.

I began by opening sacred space, then arranged seven stones from my mesa to represent the main chakras and explained them to him. He got it right away. I had a strong feeling that the work would center on his heart chakra. A pendulum confirmed this, though the throat chakra also seemed to be involved. I told him we would journey together. Going down to meet the Lord of the Lower World seemed to cause him some distress. I reiterated several times not to fear and to hold my arm if necessary. I could feel my back tightening.

My journey there is a long one, intersecting several other passages I have explored and "mapped" during years of inner-guide work. As I mentioned, I believe that there is actually a personal geography one could investigate more thoroughly, given adequate time. Thus, when I learned this particular mode of soul retrieval, it delighted me to find that the Lower World and its Keeper were simply farther and deeper than I had ventured before. But for Red Feather the passage down through bedrock, caverns, underground rivers, and a cold lake was frightening. I could feel that it took courage to continue and even more courage to trust me. When we washed up on a warm, sandy beach at a quiet bend in the river after it emerged from turbulent darkness, I realized I could see him much more clearly and that he could also see me.

He seemed relieved until I said, "I wish to introduce you in all humility to the Lord of the Lower World." For me the master of that place is as big as a tree, sometimes bigger, which is what Red Feather took him for until I directed his attention more closely.

It is worth stating here that the Lower World has little to do with the hells mentioned by various religions. Nor is its lord Satan. I have never met Satan, though it would be naïve to dismiss the existence of dark energies or to ignore our human genius for evil. And as later adventures unfolded I found that it was critical to come to terms with what I can only call the Dark. The Lord and Gatekeeper of the Lower World has other concerns, however.

What is called soul retrieval has a number of different modes and teachers and can be in any of the three worlds. I know and practice several but what follows is the way that I learned first and still find powerful. Its focus is the Lower World. Among other aspects, that is a place where wounded soul splinters find refuge, not punishment. It is sometimes described as the unconscious, though I consider that inaccurate.

In the Lower World it is possible to visit four chambers of a soul. These chambers are named Wounds, Contracts, Grace, and Treasures, each entered only with permission of the Keeper of the Lower World. He does have a name, and on occasion I have met him in a female aspect. He has also told me there is a fifth chamber named Regret, but I have yet to explore it. In addition, he has shown me an even deeper layer, a place of great thirst and desolation where I have worked on several occasions.

My vision of the Lower World is that of an endless wild garden filled with fragrant flowers, vines, and subtropical trees. Its sound is that of flowing waters, the buzzing of many insects, and the calls of exotic birds. While there is light and warmth, I have never been able to find the sun. Sometimes I can see a forest-covered mountain in the distance, a volcano perhaps. In soul retrieval, a shaman journeys for himself or another and brings back the missing soul piece in its healed state along with any other gifts that might want to return for reintegration. Missing pieces often have to do with trauma or wounding, frequently from childhood but sometimes from another lifetime. A recipient often has the strange experience of being deeply seen, like having had someone rummage through one's basement. I have learned never to presuppose what I might find or rationalize out what I see. It only diminishes the power of the work.

Ignoring Red Feather's shock at this initial meeting, I got right down to business with the Keeper.

He listened impassively and finally interrupted me. "Not so fast. Let us smoke." He manifested a pipe, already lit, and sat down hugely. We did the same, forming a triangle.

"I understand this," Red Feather immediately responded. "It is the way of my people."

Now came my turn to be surprised. I'd never seen such a thing here. The pipe passed slowly and wordlessly.

At last the Keeper said he understood exactly why we had come and that he agreed to the request we were about to present, but first he had some stern words for me. What had I brought him? I replied that I hadn't thought to bring anything. He proceeded to admonish me that if I wanted to keep coming down there, I'd need to honor his help more. We agreed this would be by putting a big piece of turquoise to represent him in my medicine bundle.

A few more puffs and we moved to the Chamber of Wounds. I couldn't make it out at first, but Red Feather knew the scene well. For me it slowly resolved into a picture of a small Indian boy on a river-bank, weeping. Whether through an attack, an epidemic, or famine, it seemed his entire village had been killed. I saw smoldering fires and a few bodies in winter twilight.

"That is me," Red Feather said. I knew he had been rescued by other relatives and had grown up with a medicine person—an uncle or cousin—but the little boy understood nothing except the feeling of being completely alone. He wished to come with us.

In the Chamber of Contracts, I saw Red Feather bound to the land, specifically the Anasazi land of southern Utah. I had proceeded carefully, with as much invisibility as I could muster, mindful that there could well be sorcery, but somehow it seemed connected with a death ritual. He seemed bound there as a guardian and protector. There were cords to specific landmarks, each of which had great emotional meaning. It seemed to me that it would be better to replace the contract represented by the specific geography with an awareness that he was now a protector of the entire planet, which I explained to him. He understood, and I left it at that. Later he told me that many more were also bound the same way.

In the Chamber of Grace, I watched the little boy from the Chamber of Wounds become the man: Red Feather in his power, sitting in the sun at the mouth of a cliff overhang with a dwelling inside. There were different birds around him and he was practicing his bird magic, taking joy in listening to their news and seeing things through their eyes. I also saw him welcoming the dawn and drawing power from a deep connection to the sun and the Earth. Then came pictures of him doing a sweat and healing people. I couldn't help asking him whether he had incurred the jealousy of the Anasazi sorcerers. He said yes, but reiterated that the best protection was confidence in his own power and connection to Spirit. That others saw his integrity as a threat just made him laugh. I got a picture of psychic arrows bouncing off him or passing through.

In the Chamber of Treasures, I saw nothing at all, just a gray color. I called on Spirit and the Keeper to help me see and suddenly saw another cliff grotto, this time with no structure. In the sandy floor at the center I saw a pipe made of whitish stone, with a feather for each of the directions.

Red Feather went to it immediately and said, "This is sacred breath." He seemed delighted.

I didn't think to ask him what it was for. As we were leaving I asked the Keeper if there might be a power animal that wished to come with us. A big, red-tailed hawk landed on Red Feather's left forearm. I understood that it had to do with both far-sightedness and invisibility, as the hawk is able to disappear into the sun.

Emerging into the Middle World, Red Feather was ebullient. He seemed grateful for my guide services. I told him it was my honor to share what little I knew. I blew the healed man—the one who no longer carried a wound story—into the stone representing his heart chakra, the pipe into the throat chakra, and the hawk into his brow. He told me that a pipe might one day come into my world for us both to use and that it would be an important sign.

The next morning I reflected on the contract chamber. Perhaps something more than a simple discussion was in order. I did not sense resistance and so simply envisioned the scene there again. This time I saw sand drawings of his local landscape with lines to each landmark. I consulted Red Feather and then erased the picture, replacing it with a circle to represent the globe. I also brought to mind a picture of the planet from space and explained my sense that helping Mother Earth was our common road now. To myself I wondered whether an aspect of our road might be to release other spirits bound in the same way, if they wished.

)

Five months later I was at a conference in Sacramento as part of my publishing work. For several days there I had felt a very strong Indian presence. Perhaps it was simply an energetic echo, for it would have been a fine place to live. But late one afternoon as I was sitting in a meeting I suddenly "saw" a delegation of eight or nine Indians. They had a head-man and were there to see Red Feather, not me. I asked Red Feather to wait until I could get back to my hotel room.

That night I was watching television when the same delegation re-turned. I sat on the edge of the bed, eyes closed, and "watched" as the spirit people calmly petitioned Red Feather for help. They were aware of me but focused on him. By then, Red Feather and I had journeyed to all the five upper worlds, the lower ones, and many places in the Middle World. He knew the paths yet said he could not journey with-out my help—at least not yet. I sometimes invited him to my personal inner world to meet my inner guide and archetypes, but he seemed to find it a bit too personal or perhaps overwhelming.

I have a practice for helping deceased human and animal spirits who have not crossed over in which I simply open a tunnel of light. They may choose to move into it. Most do, once they release their fear or panic, but there is never coercion. Very often a welcoming figure is just inside, just as I have described earlier. Afterwards there is a brief sense of lightness and release. Red Feather had observed this on nu-merous occasions. Together we opened a portal. I could see a figure.

There were others farther back. The delegation hesitated. Red Feather sent them reassurance. Slowly they moved into the opening; it closed, leaving only a sweet feeling. The strong sense of ancestral Indian presence diminished rapidly. Red Feather seemed as awestruck as I was.

)

His general disposition was very even tempered. Only rarely did I sense emotion other than quiet amusement. Once, early in our connection, I was on a flight that was passing through very unsettled air right after take off. The plane was full of tension, and I could feel apprehension from him too.

"What are you afraid of?" I asked. "You're already dead!"

There was a slight pause and then loud laughter in my ear.

Another instance is worth mentioning. A few years on, I was in a workshop conducted by the same teacher who had helped me earlier. Red Feather and I were now very comfortable with our arrangement. I was so used to his presence that I rarely gave our situation much thought. During an interlude the teacher asked whether I would mind sharing my experience with the group. I agreed and described it briefly when he invited me to do so. Most of the participants were used to hearing things of this nature and took it as a point of interest. But one of the newer ones, emphatically self-described as an anthropologist, approached me at the next break and questioned my right to keep a "pet Indian spirit" for my amusement. I wasn't sure what to say, but I could feel anger rising strongly in Red Feather.

"She knows nothing!" he shouted in my inner ear.

I did not convey his words to her, even though he demanded, "Tell her that!" Afterward I felt him sulking.

Sometime later, he told me that he didn't understand the term "Native American," though he deeply appreciated the familiar energy at pow-wows and similar events we attended on occasion. At those times, his joy and recognition could be so overwhelming that it brought tears to my eyes too. But he also told me that the great wound-story he saw was one he didn't share. I asked him whether he had names for the groups of his time and he said yes, of course, but that it was a source of division and trouble. He simply preferred to call his original group and all others "the people" in order to distinguish them from the non-human nations of beings.

And there is a final item. At the onset of all this, my wife was getting used to the idea. I told her that Red Feather walked on my left side.

She thought for a minute and then said, "So, in bed, I sleep on your left side. What about when we…?"

I could feel Red Feather tense immediately and declare, "I am a man of honor!"

Still, we soon switched bedsides.

11

Snake Energy

-May-
New Moon in Gemini

The lunar cycle passed slowly. By now I was much engaged with the changes I had initiated in my life, closing out one career and starting another whose outline seemed defined more by a sense that the journey was as important as the goal. How easy it seemed, although I had deep misgivings regarding the way things would certainly go for my organization and former employees. There was a dream-like quality to it and an odd sensation of combined speed and inertia, rather like being shot from a cannon in slow motion. No strange visitors appeared in my inner world, yet there was something odd.

The day before the new moon, I was with walking with Aquila through a forest when we stopped short at the same moment. At the base of a pine, three stone spear points were arranged as if on a clock face, pointing outward at three, six, and nine o'clock as we approached. The three o'clock was white, the six was red, and the nine was black. I made a note to return.

Coming to this place at the new moon with Red Feather, we stopped for a closer look. Not having a detailed knowledge of point typology, the best I could say was that they were Clovis — ten to twelve thousand years old. But that gave me a clue.

Observing them carefully, Red Feather said, "It is a summons."

We moved farther up the valley to what I now thought of as the Traveler's place, although he was not there. Red Feather knelt to touch the ashes of the little fire — the classic move.

"Warm," he said, not quite understanding my amusement.

From there we journeyed to the cave in the crystal mountain. It was daytime — perhaps late morning. Sea mist was rising up the valley.

Snake Energy

The skies were overcast. Five were already present when we entered. Arrow leaned into his fire, trying to get it steady. Instead of a constant green flame, it flared with red streaks and bursts. He focused his intent, uttering words under his breath. It seemed that the red was not for any lack of skill. At last he leaned back, settling for an occasional jet of red amid the green. Others had been arriving.

Suddenly he turned to me. "Nice shirt."

I had made an effort this time to be conscious of the white ceremonial buckskin shirt, given to me by the Paleolithic hunters I encountered at my sister-in-law's place the previous year. Her ranch, a few miles from Hell Gap in Wyoming, was definitely "thin" and from all indications seemed to have a long ceremonial history. I suspected the hunters were the ones who had left or sent the spear points.

Last to arrive was the woman who sat on Arrow's right. We sat silent for a while before Arrow told us to join hands. As on the last occasion, we felt the energy rising and an increase in our vibration. It came from Arrow, who seemed to be serving as a transformer. This time we went past our previous limit. I could feel him approaching, backing away, then pushing into a new level. In an instant, there was a great, reticulated serpent surrounding and encoiling us with a cool but luminous presence. I felt an unflinching gaze neither compassionate nor pitiless but absolutely literal. Arrow reduced the amplitude and the presence faded. We broke the circle.

"Snake energy is the first of the great organizing principles we encounter when we raise our vibration," he said. "It has other forms and names, but this is how we will approach it. Do not think of it and others we will touch in terms of good and bad. Now, a snake has certain interesting aspects, especially the ability to discard a skin it has outgrown. The process can be difficult, but what choice does it have? The key is that once a snake has shed what it no longer needs it does not look back." He paused. "It is time for the Earth to shed her skin — past time. We must help her, yet what would this look like?"

It was difficult to picture. We were silent. Then an image came to us. As the Earth pursued her orbit, turning every side to the sun in the course of a day, circled in turn by the moon, it seemed as if she spun out of a filmy membrane, emerging fresher and brighter, leaving the after-image to dissolve like smoke.

"Please join hands again," said Arrow. "We will touch serpent energy to help our Mother."

Our vibration rose to the previous level and then surpassed it. Once again we were enveloped in that pure archetypal energy. Unbidden, we turned our attention to our planet. Now it became obvious that she did indeed need to step out of an old skin, that she was bound and constricted by a form that had once served well but now was agony. Directing the snake energy flowing through us, we gave shape to a new, unformed becoming. The energy had its own logic and purpose. We watched enthralled as our beautiful planet stepped out of shrouds and into radiance. Arrow reduced the energy level and we broke the circle again.

"Remember to run energy in your own physical bodies while your consciousness is here in this cave," he said.

I looked at the woman to my left. She smiled. She was small, energetic, with dark hair beginning to show strands of silver.

"I am Emeen," she said.

I realized she was Middle Eastern rather than Hispanic and replied specifically in Arabic with my own name and a few of the formulaic yet nuanced responses that so fill Arab social exchange.

She smiled again. "Well, since you know my language, I will call you Kateeb."

It was a variation on the word "scribe." I liked that.

"Here you are in a cave," she continued, "just like the ancient prophets, being told to record what comes to you."

We both laughed.

"Nothing so beautiful," I replied.

I looked around. Others were also chatting.

"Many of you have been experiencing or initiating great personal changes," Arrow said abruptly. "It flows in part from the work you do here and is inevitable. Do not resist. It is also the result of your dreaming. Many on Earth also feel the results of your efforts. Let us therefore envision and strengthen that golden mist surrounding our Mother and all whom she sustains."

When we had done so, he turned to the Amazonian. "How are your trees?"

"They live," our friend replied, and for the first time showed a beautiful set of teeth in a wide smile. Everyone sat back a little and shared his satisfaction.

"The male will take longer, but he lives," he said, still smiling. "Thank you."

We sat quietly, enjoying the living picture he showed us.

"Does anyone have something to say?" asked Arrow.

People shifted and then the African woman said, "Yes, I do. In my village there is an old man. Generations of children have learned wisdom at his feet. I myself was one of them and profited from his words and example. But now no children come. His knowledge of life and its sources have little value in eyes that are wide with desire for the shiny things they see on satellite television. He grows weary. There are many more like him. My question is this: who will sustain the keepers of wisdom?"

We stared into the fire. Indeed, who would keep the wisdom keepers?

Finally Arrow said, "We will fortify their hearts. The market for wisdom is weak these days, but such times have come and gone before. The keepers must remember that what they hold is eternal and that these other distractions are ephemeral."

We joined hands and with her picture of the village elder before us sent renewed Spirit connection to his heart and all like him. Shortly we saw him brighten. And then we saw what he saw: a shy but curious little face peeping around the open door. He winked at it.

We were done. Nodding to Emeen and Arrow, I got up with Red Feather and exited the cave. There was much to do that day, and this was just the start.

12

Trouble

-June-
New Moon in Cancer

As the new moon approached I had no sense of being called, nor did I feel particularly eager to journey to the crystal mountain. I checked with my medicine bundle several times regarding the best time and got little or no response. Still, I felt it was very important to make the effort. The new moon only lasts two-and-a-half days in a sign, but the strongest response I got was a very weak one for the night of the last full day or the next morning.

It was my last week in the old job. I had worked to leave things in good order, yet my practice was already beginning to fill some evenings—including the last night of this new moon. It would be the following morning then.

During client work that evening, I had a moment to send out a power animal for a quick check. It returned almost immediately with one word.

"Trouble."

"How bad could it be?" I asked myself, rolling out of bed very early the next morning. I thought maybe something had happened to one of the Council members and he or she was unable to attend. Yet when Red Feather and I began journeying a stronger sense of danger took hold.

"Watch my back," I said to him.

"Always."

In my valley the morning sun shone off the many mountain peaks. On our right the sheer-sided guardian rose against the sky. Slightly behind us on the same side a volcano of almost constant fire stood apart in the distance, its smoke and ash drifting northeasterly in the still air. As ever, my protector was there at the valley rim.

Turning to him, I asked, "Can you accompany us to the place of our Council? We may need you."

"Of course."

Aquila, when we met him, remained motionless but met my eyes. "Be careful."

We journeyed to the cave. Instead of arriving right at the mouth I stayed quite some distance off near a crag higher on the opposite side of the sharp valley below. I sent a thought to the protector that we both needed to be cloaked in shadow. Then I stopped my thoughts and remained still. Best to wait and observe. Things felt wrong. It was morning. A winter fog from the ocean moved up the valley, dissipating as it rose. The sun highlighted fantastic arms and fingers in the rising mist, but both the cave and our vantage were well above. Several small figures emerged from the cave, though I could not tell their identities. They milled and seemed undecided.

Where was Arrow?

Suddenly they vanished. Two larger and darker figures much like my protector arced out of the mist. I held my breath. They gave a quick look into the cave then slowly merged into the morning shadows near the cave mouth. It took more memory than sight to separate their shapes from the other shades. Except for the fog, the canyon seemed devoid of any movement.

Just as suddenly the two dark shapes became evident again and shot off in different directions. My impression was that they served two different masters working in tandem. In the space of that thought I saw Arrow streaking toward the cave mouth like a comet from a point higher than ours but somewhat down canyon. It seemed best to do the same. We arrived right behind him, barely ahead of most of the others who must also have been watching. A crowd of us squeezed to get in. I took my place with Red Feather. My protector remained outside, according to the rules. Last to arrive by just a few seconds was Alice.

"Close the entrance," Arrow said to her.

At her back, the cave mouth darkened and disappeared leaving us in blackness lit only by our own faint glow. There was a strong sense of relief, but no one said a word. What had happened?

When a bit of time had passed and people began to feel calmer, Arrow caused his little fire to burst into life. It burned a steady green.

I looked around but few met my eyes. Most seemed to be still processing the event, considering what it might mean.

At last Arrow spoke. "You were wondering when to meet, but I could not issue the call. It would have further alerted those who now seek to stop us."

I felt uneasy. What had been a nice monthly prayer circle now took on a new aspect. How far into our daily lives did this danger extend?

He turned his head, gauging the effect of his words, then continued. "They seek us, but there are few who have this power, fewer still who use it in such a way, and there are many places to search." He paused again. Everything was shifting.

"We are a threat. There are certain ones whose interests lie in other directions who would like to stop us. More than stop us…," he trailed off softly and then resumed, "It has ever been so, yet I did not foresee it happening so soon or I would have warned you. We must all use caution now."

We absorbed his words. I do not think it crossed anyone's mind to request a release. Quite the contrary, it added an element of seriousness to our work but also an element of interest. I considered the mechanics of protection and the logistics of our meetings. If our work hinged on maintaining a quorum of thirteen, then we might need to look out for each other as much as ourselves. Yet I wasn't quite prepared to consider how serious our opposition might be.

"Let us center our circle," Arrow said with a smile. "Bring yourselves here. We have work to do."

It was good to feel the rising energy of our group, bringing us back to the present and to our purpose.

"Now send the Earth our love," he said.

We bathed her in golden mist, affirming the newly emerged beauty we had helped from our previous session. When we broke the circle, the events of our arrival seemed remote.

"We will meditate on our moon, our beautiful lady," said Arrow.

I was surprised, but then I realized the timing was perfect.

"We can never know all her ways," Arrow continued, "nor does she expect us to. But consider her cycle from new moon, the time of beginnings, to fullness and the time of fruition and celebration, to the remnant moon and the time of reflection. Consider her deep connection with the waters of our Mother and our personal ebb and flow. Send her your deep blessings!"

We linked hands. In some ways it felt like a relief to me. Here was a mystery that didn't need exploring. She could inform us, or not. Our part was simply to extend gratitude for her beauty.

When the circle broke, I looked at the doorway. It remained perfectly dark. I now recognized everyone and noted some of the members who had seemed less clear to me. Some returned my gaze; others focused inwardly.

Without words, we joined our hands again. The issue on everyone's mind was planetary warming.

Arrow only said, "What we do, we do to ourselves. We make it warmer still." He let the thought expand, then added, "Instead, bring consciousness into the relationship of the humans to the Earth. It is a new way of being, the way of the future."

As he painted this picture, I saw a new circle opening, one in which humans brought the Earth into their considerations, but also one in which the Earth responded more directly and immediately. The vision was immense and it echoed as far into the future as I could see and cannot be contained in these words. "Purity of reciprocity" or "balance of mutual good intent" might be places to start, but "mutual recognition of consciousness" might be as important. Perhaps there is a better human language than English for such concepts.

We focused on this grand picture, and I could feel Arrow charging our circle, raising the vibration effortlessly past anything we had done before. At a certain point we felt the Earth awaken as if from a deep sleep, looking around, asking, "How long has it been since we walked together?" It went far beyond ordinary notions of harmony, opening into a new potential of growing together. That would truly be walking in beauty, I thought to myself. The vision and the vibration could only be sustained for so long, but we ended by sending out love to all. I added family members, friends, and pets as well. When we broke our circle and our vibration dropped, I found it increasingly difficult to retain memory of the immense purity I had witnessed.

Now there was different business.

Without a trace of smile, Arrow brought us around quickly. "Leave slowly in ones and twos. Call your protectors. You all have them. It is one of the reasons you are here."

I had to smile a little at the thought of twelve or thirteen of these large, mysterious, lightless figures hanging around the cave mouth like a bunch of smokers on a break. No one seemed to share my amusement.

Several people rose immediately and slipped through the small opening Alice created just as they headed out. The day was bright and each sliver of light was blinding. Finally only Arrow, Red Feather, Alice, and I remained. I held back because I wanted words with her.

At the exit, I stopped and introduced myself as the husband of one of her students.

"Ah, so you're the one."

My wife had recently decided to stop studying with her, in part because the path seemed increasingly harsh. I said so now.

"Ah," she said again. "Perhaps I pushed her too hard. I felt she had greater potential than many and wished for her to learn things well. I am sorry. Please tell her so. But I am also happy that you and I share this work."

I nodded, and she opened the curtain of darkness for Red Feather and me.

We shot right out, joined by the protector, but instead of moving directly to our starting point we curved out over the ocean fog bank. Slowing a little, I immediately sensed more than saw the approach of the two watchers. We dropped into the fog, not knowing whether it would make any difference. I wanted to ask the protector about it, but it was best course to be still in body and thought, surrounded by his shadow. After a time I could feel the watchers move off. I made a note to ask later whether they homed on thoughts or motion or something else. In the short term it seemed best not to experiment.

We had already raised the stakes.

13

The Jinn

~June-July~

"And He created jinn from fire free of smoke."
—Qur'an, 55:15

I had to know. What was the nature of these things? What was the level of danger?

The next time I visited my valley, I quizzed my protector. A few years before, he, or it, just appeared on the edge of the inner world and told me he had been "given" to me. I checked this as soon as I could with Amun, who confirmed everything.

"It's up to you to use him as you choose. We thought you might be ready," he said with the hint of a smile.

I understood this went well beyond a nice present. It was a test.

The entity most closely resembled one of those blocky, horned figures so common to the ancient rock art in the area where I lived. It certainly gave new meaning to the images when I encountered them on desert canyon walls or in photographs. Mostly he seemed to be a huge wall of shadow, ten feet or higher.

He told me immediately that rather like the Los Angeles police department his mission was to protect and serve. I liked that. He also said that he could "find things," that he would always walk on my right, and that he was capable of moving in the entire Middle World and even the higher segments of the Lower World. I never detected any emotion. In fact, I couldn't even see his eyes—if there were any.

I began carefully by asking whether he could find me better eyesight. He took me back to a time in grade school in the Midwest when I was just realizing that I needed glasses. Now, instead of squinting at the blackboard, I followed him out the building and down to the marsh on a glorious autumn day. I did what eight-year-old boys do in marshes, catching frogs, creeping through reed tunnels, getting gloriously muddy. And then we passed even deeper into the countryside to a hill where he told me to focus on things such as distant leaves and ants on tree bark. I returned with him a number of times. We encountered a special horse and went even farther to meet magic bison. And there was the encounter with that fellow named Anton. As far as I could tell, my eyesight never changed, but the trips were always interesting and at first seemed to have a lot to do with stepping away from segmented time. He never explained things, however, and my questions generated very little in the way of additional information. Once I asked him if he was the gatekeeper of the Lower World.

"I am not!" he replied.

Really, I was just checking, for I deduced fairly quickly that he was probably a *jinn*.

This particular one, who remained nameless, also seemed able to make small sums of money turn up, if I specified them. Once he located an item I had misplaced in the house. These seemed poor uses, however, and I found them distracting. Of greater interest were his protective abilities. I discovered I could ask him to watch over a pet or a loved one if I felt they were open to danger.

One day, walking across the university for a meeting, I idly asked what else he could do.

"I can envelop you in shadow for invisibility," he replied.

"Do it," I said." Instantly I felt a thin, dark fog surround me. People passing suddenly seemed only vaguely aware of my presence, though it hardly constituted proof of anything. I continued to work with his veil, and found it quite useful in places such as airports. It also worked in the inner world. I was certain of another thing: if I asked him to harm another creature, he would have done so just as easily.

)

It had not occurred to me that others might also have jinn, but perhaps that was simply because so much went on in my inner-world journeys that I never had time to fully explore every possibility. Seeing those dark shapes at the cave mouth, coupled with Arrow's admonition, made me realize I was heedless not to have considered the idea. In fact some people would certainly view the jinn as excellent tools for darker ends.

Usually "my" jinn's response to questions came in one or two words. Sometimes I got an entire sentence. Now my question elicited the longest conversation we had ever had. The two shadows at the cave mouth were sent by two people working together, not one. Jinn key on shadows more than physical forms and derive a great deal of information from them. Twilight times are preferred because shadows are longest, but jinn can move at all times of the day, particularly night. They can easily recognize luminous forms in darkness. I asked whether jinn could perceive other jinn. Yes, but they can also choose to be almost unseen by one another. My jinn seemed unperturbed by events, yet his answers only generated more questions.

I took it up with Amun.

"The interests of jinn and humans coincide very little," he said. "There are three ways that jinn work with humans. First, they can choose to do so. That is rare. Second, they can be enslaved. Solomon was good at that," he said, musing distantly in a way I had never seen. We were silent for a moment before he returned his gaze to mine. "Third, and most common, they consent to be gifted. It is a test for both parties."

"What happens when they attack?"

"They do not strike a killing blow in an earthly sense. You would feel you had been cut off from Source and would wither. Like being enveloped in deep despair. Very sad, very unpleasant. Eventually it can be fatal. A lot would depend on your own sense of connection. The best defense against anything of the sort is simply joyful affirmation of your connection to Spirit, of course."

I thought of the dementors in the Harry Potter books.

"Something like that," he said, "but more individual. They do have names, which are hard to obtain."

)

Arrow had told us to use our protectors, our jinn. I asked mine to guard the house at night and to warn me if there was anything immediate. The month passed with me deeply involved in my own life changes. I was generally untroubled by the implications of the events at the cave mouth and barely thought of them for days at a time. One day, when I did remember, I asked the jinn whether there had been any attacks.

"Several," he said. "I deflected them."

A few nights later, I awoke, sensing something at the front door. I realized that the jinn was standing squarely before it as two dark shadows dove at him repeatedly from the air. Waves were beating against a standing stone, will against will. One of my dogs began to bark in his sleep. Then everything subsided. I thanked the jinn, as I had done many times, but as always he indicated that thanks were unnecessary. Far from being scared, I was intrigued.

I went hiking in the mountains several days after that. About to emerge from the forest onto a broad meadow, I stopped at the margin, something Red Feather had taught me.

I heard the jinn say, "Practice invisibility."

Without thinking I felt his shadow envelop my two dogs and me. I saw nothing ahead but called on one of my other options too before stepping out, careful to keep my mind clear of thoughts. I felt a searching gaze and then something swept down the meadow and back. The presence lingered, but I kept up my pace. It was early afternoon, quite hot.

"It is hard for them to see you because at this time of day you cast almost no shadow," my jinn said.

The whole thing seemed somewhat matter of fact, until I reviewed it later.

)

As the new moon approached I began to wonder how the Council would meet.

One day during my morning meditation Aquila said, "He's here," meaning the Traveler.

We went to the meeting place. He was standing there, wearing summer gear of brown leather, waiting. We both nodded in greeting.

"The Council will meet one day later than usual. Do not travel there. Meet me here that evening and I will guide you."

"Good," I said. It eased some of my concern. "Who are you?" I asked, seizing the opportunity.

Aquila approached him more closely, took a few sniffs, and seemed to relax a little.

The Traveler smiled. "I live on Earth as you do. I am a hunter, and I guide people and bring them together for common purpose. You might say that I hunt connections and possibilities." He looked down. "I think your wolf is starting to like me."

Aquila had settled close to the Traveler but was pointedly looking away.

Leaving the Traveler, we retraced our steps down valley through the trees, keeping the stream on our right.

"He can be trusted," Aquila said, "but I still don't like him just showing up like that."

I suppressed a laugh, thinking that most of the dogs I had known harbored lingering suspicion regarding the person who delivered the mail. I wondered whether to rename our guest the Postman.

14

Thirst

~July~
New Moon in Leo

The new moon reached the far edge of its sign. Red Feather and I journeyed at night to the rim of the hanging valley where we collected the jinn and then descended to meet Aquila. At the encounter, Red Feather sat on his heels, looking sideways into the wolf's eyes without touching him.

"You never cease to amaze me," he finally said, turning to me.

Earlier, he had told me that medicine people of his time worked years to gain the assistance of the sort of helpers and allies who seemed to come to me almost unbidden. I suggested that perhaps the barriers between worlds now were simply thinner, which made it easier for us in this regard, but he seemed unconvinced.

The four of us went up the valley. We knew the Traveler would be waiting and soon could see his little fire through the trees. As soon as we burst into the circle of light, he rose and scuffed out the burning twigs.

"Stay close to me," he said.

Aquila retreated to the edge of the trees, while the rest of us rose in the air. The Traveler guided us to a beach I recognized as one on the coast not many miles from the Crystal Cave. The two African members of the Council were there. I wondered if the Traveler had brought them too. We greeted each other with hugs and then the Traveler led us all through the air almost at ground level toward the cave. For a moment I could see the African man's jinn moving right beside him.

At the edge of the mountains we slowed and began fading from one jagged boulder on the valley floor to another. When the cave entrance—or the place where we knew it to be—was barely in view, we stopped to watch. After a few minutes there was a tiny gleam of light from the cave, so fast it would have gone unnoticed if we had not been focused on that spot. Without hesitating we shot up to the cave a mile or more distant and a thousand feet higher. The rest of the Council was already assembled, but the members sat in darkness. The Traveler remained inside by the entrance for a minute, peering out, and then vanished. Arrow nodded. The two members closest to the opening moved together, sealing it with blackness. I knew that outside there were many shadowy protectors.

Another minute passed in absolute darkness, then a small, green flame sprang up before Arrow, growing to the diameter of two hands. I engaged each member silently. The mood was sober, but I felt fear from no one. We linked hands. The month had been interesting for all, and our stories circulated wordlessly with the rising energy. Eventually we released the circle, but still no one spoke.

At last Arrow raised his gaze from the fire for the first time and scanned the green-lit faces. "The world is on fire. There is war, heat. Fear creates thirst, yet in their fear people drink even more deeply from that cup. We will send cool waters to all of humanity, thirsty for Spirit."

We linked and felt the energy rising in us, around us, then moving faster and faster in the circle of our joined hands. I felt serpent energy rise and then we moved to an even higher level of a completely different texture. From my training I recognized it as jaguar energy, but it continued to rise until we touched an even higher resonance.

There was a rush of wind and noise. A great torrent of crystal-blue water poured through the center of our circle within inches of our crossed legs. The air in the chamber filled with moisture and spray. I pictured it raining on upturned faces in the world's desperate places, filling the hearts and souls of warring and suffering peoples with drops of the Divine, lifting them briefly above the rationalizations bred by fear. We held it as long as we could, longing to open our own mouths to drink deeply yet holding the greater purpose. When we began to flag, the energy dropped, the water vanished, and the fire was burning as sweetly as before.

We were silent, awed by the beauty and power of what we had

seen. As the image faded, Arrow spoke to the question that was on a few minds.

"Those who seek to hinder us? Do not engage them; do not fear. In this, you have all done well. Some of them believe that the world must end before it can begin again. They seek to hasten its demise. Others believe that the darkness and pain within themselves must be extended to all. Still others believe they can profit from chaos while standing apart from its effects. As you have seen, some among them are powerful sorcerers or have sorcerers doing their bidding. Let us send love to those who wish us ill. If nothing else it will confuse them!" He laughed.

We linked again, opening our hearts.

When we broke the circle, Arrow said, "Let's sing a song. I know a good one!" He began a melody whose only words were *heya heya hey hey*.

Almost instantly everyone joined because it was a song we all knew somehow. It felt good. Smiles broke out.

Shortly, Arrow stopped and said loudly, "Socialize!"

People stood up slowly and began moving about the small cave as if at a cocktail party.

I went quickly to Alfred across the floor. We had just completed a training together during which I had the opportunity to quiz him about the Council. He said he had no knowledge of it, but people told him from time to time that they had encountered him in dreamtime and he had no reason to doubt them. Now I wanted to talk to him on this side.

"It was good to see you," he said simply. "Let's try to work together soon."

Paqo and Alice remained at the door. Paqo said, "Come back to my country soon. We'll walk in the mountains again together. We'll go to Vilcabamba!"

Alice sent greetings and love to my wife.

The Amazonian said, "I can see that you have been to the plant world and that a strong plant medicine has befriended you. There is much to learn from him, if you honor him and let him teach you. If you are ever in my jungle, I can help you with that."

I returned to my place. Emeen had just seated herself too.

"Are you safe?" I asked. There was another war in her part of the world.

"*Al-hamdu lillah*, war has not touched us, yet," she replied, "though it is not far away."

"How did you get your jinn?" I asked, wondering if this was polite and laughing at myself a little.

She seemed eager to talk, however. "It came to me in a dream and said it was given to me. When I awoke I knew it was a good thing, but still I prayed for guidance in making use of its powers. I do believe it is female."

I was delighted, but everyone had resumed places and Arrow looked ready to begin again.

"How many times have we met?" he asked the Chinese fellow.

"Seven."

"Ah. It is time to begin what we are really here for, dreaming the world into being." He was silent for a moment, looking around the cave at us each with total engagement. "Let us join hands. Let our energy rise to the level you attained earlier tonight and beyond. From there we will follow the lines."

Through joined hands we felt the connection, the flow, and the rising harmonic, passing our earlier high mark and pushing even higher into a place of vision. I understood what Arrow had meant about the lines. From where we sat, seemingly fixed in time and space, we could see lines of possibility, or destiny, along which our Earth and our human race could proceed. Immediately before us the lines were tightly bunched, but as they stretched out farther some lines began to veer off gently. A few diverged radically. Some peeled off and then re-crossed others father out. Yet in the very far distance, beyond human comprehension and our ability to follow, it seemed that the lines all converged. We followed some, and the action was like plucking a harp string. The simple act of observing activated a line and its possibilities. Some were alarming. There was a desert planet; a place of sand and extreme dryness populated by a few wanderers whose half-believed ancient legends spoke of a time when water flowed freely. There was a vision of the Earth as a hot, smoldering stone, completely uninhabited. There was also a vision of a green, steamy, jungle planet, ruled by plants and a suffocating green consciousness. I felt Arrow calling us back from our wanderings.

There was another path, difficult at first, a vision of Earth struggling to break through layers of scabby encrustment, like a burn victim repeatedly breaking newly formed skin to allow for greater healing. Light began to shine through the cracks in the dark and dead crust, and then in a burst of consciousness the scabs began melting away, no longer needed. As this happened we saw nations gathering in the realization of godhood and connection to Spirit that transcended ethnicity, regional identity, and creed. In this vision, Earth and humanity evolved in consciousness in a dance of mutual awareness.

Arrow spoke from a great distance. "It is hard to see past the crust to the light. These are all just seeds now, but any can grow. Let us choose this one. It is important that we all agree."

Assent flowed around the circle, and we plucked the string, watching it activate and begin vibrating. The energy we had been sustaining suddenly flowed into that path and we came back to the cave as if dropped from a height. No one spoke for a few minutes as we considered what we had seen and returned more fully to the cave. Arrow extinguished the fire.

"Remember. Do not fear. Do not engage those who seek to distract you with their 'attacks.' And keep our vision in mind." He signaled the doorkeepers to open the entrance.

A cool breeze swept in. We could see stars.

After waiting a few moments, the woman on Arrow's right shot straight out the cave mouth from her seated position and into space on a trajectory just above the mountains. A few moments more and Paqo got up, plummeting after one step off the edge. The way he did it was quite comical. I suppressed a laugh. I stood with Red Feather and did the same, dropping into the tumbled boulders at the base of the cliff face. We blended with them, aided by the protector, who seemed to have picked us up on the way down, and waited without movement or thought. High above, where the cave mouth should have been, there was nothing. A little longer, and we sank into the Earth to follow underground streams and passages back to our starting point in my own valley. It was still night, and I could see the great volcano lighting the dark with red and yellow.

"Let's go there for cleansing," I said to Red Feather.

It was a thingI often did, stepping directly into the molten fire, feeling it burn away my body in a crackling instant, which left a sensation of having been deeply cleansed.

"I cannot," he replied, and I realized that he was right.

"Then how about this stream?"

He agreed immediately. We immersed ourselves in the icy flow and let it wash over us after a night of thirsty work.

15

Fireworks

Once again, I wasn't sure when to journey. Approaches to the last several meetings of the Council were tricky affairs, but this time I sensed nothing, nor had the month seemed unusual. The wall calendar showed the basic new-moon date, but an ephemeris indicated that the new moon would not occur until late evening. I awoke early that day, considering whether to get going and drifted back into sleep.

Someone said, "We're waiting."

It was a beautiful late-summer alpine afternoon in my valley. With the protector, Red Feather and I met Aquila.

"Your friend isn't here," he said, referring to the Traveler, "but your guide wishes a word."

We went to Amun.

"Do not think you are unsought," he warned. "There are those who would stop you. Among them are people who consider themselves holders of high and worthy intent. Be cautious. If you need help do not hesitate to call on an archetype."

I had rarely if ever called in such a way on the twenty-two archetypes represented by the major arcana of the tarot, though I worked with them extensively. Mostly it was easier to get their assistance by meeting them directly in the deep inner world, always with Amun present as a buffer if necessary. The few times I tried enlisting them, unmediated, in the world of daily affairs, had been "interesting" but very difficult to contain. Something like trying to get a drink from a fire hose. Amun's words surprised me a little.

"What archetype would be good for protection?"

"Death might be suitable." He smiled.

I thanked him, and we went to Traveler's empty place. From there I set my intent to go immediately to the sharp boulder field somewhat near the base of the cliff below the crystal cave. I had already seen that a dense sea fog hung over everything. We sat quietly. Yes, there were searchers. I could feel them moving about, probing. The fog seemed to confuse them. One came near and we used our best invisibility. As it moved away, an even denser patch of fog descended. We used the opportunity to begin drifting toward the cave.

The cave was dark, seemingly unoccupied. Perhaps we were the first. I entered with Red Feather and felt as if I had passed through a barrier. In fact, everyone was present and I was the last. We took our place and sat with the Council in silence and without thought. Shortly, Arrow said a word and the green flame sprang up before him, illuminating our faces. The crystal behind him slowly came to life even more brightly.

"Welcome," Arrow said quietly, looking at each of us in turn.

We linked hands wordlessly, letting our combined energy rise effortlessly through different levels, simply allowing the flow. It was strong. When the moment seemed right, we lowered the intensity and released hands. No one spoke.

"You have held the picture from our last meeting beautifully," Arrow said at last. "Even touching that chord energizes it. Let us now energize it further."

Joining hands, we moved our energetic level up, feeling the great serpent appear again, and then sensing huge wings enfolding our circle. We focused on the same picture of a gathering of nations in Spirit after a dark time, our time, expanding it, strengthening the connection of human to Earth, human to Spirit, and from there the heartfelt connection between humans. I touched again on the thought that so much of our work to bring balance to the Earth involved human healing before losing myself in the beauty of the picture. We watched in wonder as ancient, fear-based structures and logic were abandoned, replaced by the higher logic of spiritual connection with one another, Earth, and heaven, allowing our planet to join the great choir of living planets. The poison we had all endured for so long, believing it was our only support, ebbed, slowly replaced by a language and substance of light. The inflow gathered momentum and lifted us even higher to a place where nothing really mattered. We kept the vision but saw things in an even purer form. Fireworks exploded suddenly. Living globes of light descended softly on the vision we held, illuminating even the most enshadowed heart. We directed a few of them. Some went to world leaders trapped in their mirror mazes, some to people in search of healing, some as gifts to our friends, spouses, relatives and the many nonhuman nations sharing our planet. I sent one to the Dalai Lama just for fun and heard him say, "Ho! Good one!"

It was almost too big and too strong to hold. Finally we had to let go.

Sitting in stillness, I became aware of something within me and found that the dragons I had been experiencing coming strongly into my chakras since June were fully alive and energized.

Arrow raised his head and turned toward me. "Look! Scribe has seven dragons! He even thinks there might be a black one."

I felt everyone's gaze but was too wrapped in the intense sensations to return their attention.

"What *are* they?" I asked after a few moments. It was a question I had puzzled ever since the first one appeared more than a year before.

"Let them tell you," he laughed. "But you already know that on one level they are rays that match those of your energy centers."

I did already know that and guessed there were more, perhaps as many as five, that were not within my power to perceive but might be accessed through a black one. I focused on my internal process briefly. Raising my eyes, I saw that others had as many as three or four dragons of their own and were experiencing similar sensations. When I looked at Arrow I could see he had seven. He grinned.

We relaxed and then without even joining hands felt each other's spirit and openness. I realized again that I could trust each of these people without reservation.

Arrow spoke. "Let the vision we have further energized pull you forward through the dark days — and there must be dark days. Put it in your medicine bundle, those of you who follow that particular way. Let people feel it in you. Let them source from the energy of your vision. It is not yours to keep secret!" He looked at each of us to emphasize the point. "Now, let us sit in gratitude to the Creator."

Through our linked hands we let the energy rise and flow of its own accord, holding only praise and gratitude in our hearts. Praise for the One who had created the infinite universes; gratitude for being able to walk in beauty this day and every day. At last we released. I felt energized, refreshed, and filled with deep stillness.

Arrow doused the fire. Light faded from the great crystal. I was unaware that anyone other than Arrow and I had said a word during the entire meeting. Perhaps there had been whole conversations.

"We will leave one by one, slowly," Arrow said. "Remember that nothing stands between you and Spirit. What you fear takes your power. This knowledge is your best protection of all." He nodded, affirming his own words.

The cave mouth came into outline, though daylight did not enter. People began to depart in order of their proximity to the entrance, one leaving to the right, one left, one down, another left, and so on. At last there were just three of us. I looked at the woman to Arrow's right and smiled. She returned the smile and I felt a connection that hadn't been there before.

"You two should meet," said Arrow, meaning in daily life.

"My name is Victoria," she said.

"Mine is…" I was about to say my given name, but Arrow interjected.

"Little Feather, the name given you by your celestial parents."

"Little Feather," I finished.

"Yes, we should meet," she said, laughing at Arrow's seriousness. Then she rose and slipped out.

Arrow and I remained—and Red Feather.

"Little Feather and Red Feather," I said. "Are you sure there is not a problem with him being here?"

"No, he is permitted. He is learning things to take back to his people."

"Then he is not dead?"

"In the strictest sense of time, of course he is dead. I don't have to explain this to you. As you also know, you have an agreement. He learns journeying from you; you learn bird magic from him. It is an honorable exchange."

I felt Red Feather nod.

We stood to leave.

"I will be here if you need to talk," said Arrow.

Stepping out the cave mouth into a gray mist, we turned left, soon joined by my protector. We headed out over the ocean, diving under the water as we on a previous occasion. I paused for bearings and felt something dark shoot by at great speed. After that, we remained motionless and resumed movement only very slowly.

When I came at last into my body, I was filled with strange sensations that lasted for several hours. It was a gorgeous morning. I went outside to admire the hummingbirds jousting at the feeders. Big clouds hung in the still sky.

16

Presence

When I awoke I knew it was time. Another bright day rose, but the news dwelled on an anniversary of the World Trade Center attacks. My head was foggy from wine. The previous evening my wife and I had hosted a birthday party, yet today I understood that I would meet the Traveler. He had been waiting several days but only said, "When you're ready." It was past time. I took my medicine bundle and on a hunch added the big crystal. Although I always kept my mesa at hand for these journeys I could not recall opening it for any. This time I did.

Pulling errant bits of consciousness back toward me, I began the work of centering, focusing on being present in my body and then present in the moment, before beginning the journey. Almost as an afterthought, I invited Red Feather to accompany me. As we traveled deeper and deeper things became more clear. I was relieved. Passing through the door to my valley, I saw that it was early evening, just past sunset. The air was cooling, and shadows were growing quickly. I asked the protector to accompany me.

Aquila waited in his usual spot. Without speaking, we made our way slowly to the Traveler's place and a small, winking fire. It occurred to me that I had never tried to make a fire in the inner world. The Traveler was working on a hunting bow but put it down when we approached.

"Bring all your friends," he said, standing.

We traveled west, crossing from night into daylight, finally arriving in a forest. There was almost no undergrowth. The trees were some kind of pine I did not know, and I sensed we were in low mountains. Somehow it also felt Asian. It was late morning, cloudless but cool.

A grassy track ran before us. We waited. Soon a group of men appeared, unmistakably bearing a shrouded corpse. They had shaven heads and wore dark robes. Monks. Perhaps the dead man needed help passing over, I thought to myself, but the Traveler sent a thought to me: no. The monks passed without heeding us. We followed.

At a clearing they stopped. A grave had been prepared. I was confused by my assumptions. No cremation? It seemed that the deceased had carried some authority, yet with little ceremony they laid the body on the ground before the grave and waited with bowed heads. Suddenly the dead man's spirit stepped out of his body and sped toward the sun. The monks raised their heads, smiled slightly, then lowered the lifeless body into the ground. Two seized shovels that laid by the raw dirt and proceeded with the burial. On completion, three monks sat on each side of the grave with one at the head. This time they did not bow their heads and kept their eyes open. I looked at the Traveler.

"So?"

"Wait. Observe."

I thought perhaps we might see the spirit return. Then I noticed that as the monks sat unmoving their etheric bodies seemed to look up and notice us for the first time. It was strange. One actually left his body and approached us. The Traveler seemed unconcerned.

"It was our Abbot's wish that we request help for that man." He nodded toward the monk seated at the head of the grave. "We have done everything in our power, but there are things we cannot do." He turned and moved back to his body.

I noticed for the first time that the monk in question alone had not shifted his etheric body. With closer scrutiny, I could see one, no, two entities within him. Now I understood.

Opening my eyes from meditation, I grasped a stone from my mesa—a seeing stone. I returned to the scene. Yes, two entities, one was the man's deceased brother, the other was something much nastier that I couldn't quite discern.

I approached slowly from the man's right. He looked quite unwell and was listing to one side. The brother's energy seemed to be lodged in the man's upper left chest. The darker entity was drawing on his life force near the navel. I sought to obscure myself, but the brother became aware of me and shifted within the man's body. I could tell now that he considered himself his brother's defender, though in fact the actual threat was well ensconced and hardly seemed concerned at all. I peered inside and saw that the dark shape lower in the body was feeding steadily from the second chakra. It had a dark, mottled, serpentine form, muscular and greasy.

Before I could determine its origin, the brother shouted, "What do you want?"

I feared he would rouse the other entity before I was ready, but apparently it was accustomed to such events. In effect the brother's efforts served to protect it as well. I had seen similar situations and sometimes wondered whether I had an affinity or if it was just some kind of unpleasant specialty.

Intrusive entities come in different forms. Sometimes it is a deceased relative, unwilling or afraid to cross into the Light, or even held back by the host's own reluctance to release them. Sometimes it is a hungry ghost, stuck between worlds. There are nastier ones, often quite conscious, that seem to be thought forms ultimately human created. But there are darker sources as well. I had never seen a positive situation, for invariably the intrusions draw life energy from their host. My own position with Red Feather seemed to be an exception. For one thing he existed outside my body.

Comparison with common notions of spirit possession would be misguided. Still, the need was to remove what didn't belong. In cases involving two or more intrusive entities I usually began with what I considered the lesser of the two, although lately I'd begun to approach the human energies as cautiously as the seemingly more parasitic but perhaps less conscious ones.

"It's time to move into the Light, Kenji," I said, for that was the inner brother's name. He had not been a monk but had encouraged his younger sibling, now elderly, to take vows, perhaps in an effort to deal with this particular situation.

"I must protect my brother from...that." He didn't exactly point, but I knew what he meant.

"If I remove it, will you then go?"

"Yes, but you will find it impossible. I have tried, as did our father, and his before him. It has followed us across generations."

Ah, I thought to myself and said to him, "Please allow me to try."

I moved closer and began scanning quietly and delicately. The darker energy was ancient. It was important to discover its origins. If someone had put it there, that person might want it to remain — even across time and generations. In fact the brother's reference to his ancestry gave me a good idea of the source. The entity stopped its slow feeding, sensing a threat. I stopped my thoughts and signaled the protector to shroud me. After a few moments it resumed its process. I opened my mind to it carefully. It was not hard to track. Somewhere in the past a young man had reneged on a marriage contract. The prospective bride's enraged family hired a sorcerer to lay a curse on the groom and his male descendants, and fathers unconsciously passed the curse to sons. After a few generations the repeating links of misfortune would have seemed merely another aspect of family identity. No doubt the story was much larger, but I had almost all the necessary information. The final question was simply whether the sorcerer had been around lately to check the handiwork. The curse was well laid, but not very subtle. No, it was a work for hire, not a sorcerer's vendetta.

I made my move.

Grasping the crystal from my bundle and holding it like a pen, I used my intent to bring it over the suffering monk's midsection and began to rotate it counterclockwise, working in two worlds at once. The green-and-black serpent raised its head in alarm and became aware of me. It coiled tighter around the man's spine. He groaned, but the crystal exercised an attractive force in several ways. The serpent, too, was cursed in that its sole and ancient task was slow destruction of the men in this line. Perhaps it once enjoyed fulfilling the purpose for which it had been created, but even that had passed beyond memory. The bright crystal offered an end to weariness. Finally it released its hold and entered the echoing facets. I did not engage it, simply being careful not to let the other end of the crystal point in my direction. It was out. I would clean the crystal later, sending the entity to the four directions with a prayer of peace and rest, or into the Dark if that was where it resonated.

I felt the brother relax. Lifting such a curse from one family member can free others, even back to the one first afflicted. The whole world smiles. Certainly the monks did.

"Now it is your turn," I said to him. "If I open a door, will you go into the Light?"

"Yes, I am weary. My thanks."

Again with my intent I visualized a great portal opening like a camera aperture. Light beamed out. A figure was just inside. I heard a rushing sound. I have mentioned the light, but when one of these opens there is also a compelling sense of home and long-sought return. The elder brother stepped out of the younger without my intervention and went toward the aperture, hesitating at first, then moving faster, seeing something so attractive it excluded everything else. He crossed the threshold and disappeared in the brightness. The portal closed in on itself and was gone. Everything seemed dark for a moment.

The monks' bodies merged ethereal with physical again. They raised their heads, smiling. The one at the head of the grave opened his eyes and looked about for the first time, as if emerging from a deep fog. One of the others turned in our direction and said out loud, "Thanks, and blessings." Whether this place coexisted with my own point in time was impossible to say, but the light in the trees and the monks' complete presence with the moment seemed more real and enduring than the rekindled rage, fear, and sadness that consumed so many on this day in the outer world.

It was time to go. But I turned first to the Traveler.

"Why does this come to me?"

"You have made yourself available."

We returned the way we came, crossing back into night. This time the Traveler accompanied us all the way to the remnants of his little fire.

"I will be back soon," he said, and was gone.

I wanted to meet Amun before going to the business of the day. Thanking the protector for his help, I went with Red Feather to meet my guide. As we neared him, Red Feather dropped to his knees and touched his head to the ground.

"Master!" he said, as he always did. Such meetings were rare, mostly because they seemed to affect my friend so deeply.

"Little Feather, you still doubt," Amun swung to me with a slight smile, using that name for the first time. "But it was well done, all the same." Then he motioned to Red Feather, who had not moved. "When will you introduce him to his guide?"

17

The Quickening

~September~
New moon in Virgo
Equinox

My protector twice stated that it would be better to journey at night at the new moon. It put me on alert. I prepared, calling in the directions, asking Spirit for help, guidance, and protection. I conferred with Red Feather, and then we journeyed.

It had been raining a cold rain, in my valley but the night sky was clearing now. I have said that the weather here generally preceded what I would experience in daily life. It wasn't long, however, before I noted that for trips to Crystal Cave the weather and time of day seemed to be exactly coincident with outer conditions. In the west, I could see the volcano's red glow above the horizon. Closer in the southwest, the protecting mountain towered above the valley as a blackness in the sky.

A long time ago, I asked my first guide where this place was. His slightly enigmatic response was all I needed to know at the time. When I learned to journey even deeper to the Lower World, meeting the Keeper there, understanding some of his names, and working with him for soul retrievals and other explorations, I discovered that the way to his world ran past the nondescript but magic portal I entered to visit my valley. Of course I had passed by my door on several occasions, venturing as far as a great subterranean lake where I met some interesting people on the far shore, but it had not occurred to me to seek the obvious: an outlet that ran even deeper.

The first time I was led to meet the Lord and Keeper of the Lower World, I was surprised but gratified to find the way went through that lake and beyond. Gratified, because it confirmed that for me at least there was a partially fixed geography to be explored if I chose. Most of the time I went through the door to my valley, simply because there was a lot to do, and the vast, shifting realms I encountered there in the course of working with the powerful archetypes contained much information and offered many treasures.

Yet a few days before, I chanced to ask Amun the relation of his world to the Lower World. I had concluded that it was part of the Lower World, sort of like an upstairs apartment.

"This is not the Lower World," he said emphatically. "This is part of the Middle World, your world. The only way to the Lower World is past its guardian."

Now things made more sense.

At the rim of the valley we met the protector and then went to meet Aquila.

"The Traveler is not here," Aquila said. "I will take you to his fire circle, but I will not go farther."

It was the first time he had called the Traveler by name, rather than "he" or "that man."

I probably didn't need to begin at the Traveler's place, but it was habit now, one that helped anchor the beginning and end of each occasion. From there, Red Feather, the jinn, and I journeyed to the jumbled rocks at the cliff base, this time in a different spot relative to the cave mouth. What I saw startled me. High on the smooth face, bright light spilled out. Was it a trick? I was mindful of the protector's cautions. We watched. Soon two figures seemed to materialize at the entrance and enter. Still suspicious I waited a little longer but sensed no danger.

We raced toward the cave, pausing at its lip, ready for anything. Arrow was seated with two others. They greeted us warmly. I took my place with Red Feather. Then there was a great crowding at the door. It seemed everyone else was waiting and watching too. Now they were laughing and pushing to get to their places. Arrow was in high spirit and had a huge fire going, although when all were in place he motioned for the door to be sealed.

"Your work is already effective," he said immediately.

"What about those who sought to stop us?" asked the woman seated between the Amazonian and the Chinese fellow. She voiced the common question.

"Remember that they too believe they are doing right. They do not understand our motives, and our work has already passed beyond the comprehension of some of them. For the moment they do not consider us a threat," he said, before emphasizing quietly, "for now."

We joined hands to harmonize our energy, letting it rise on its own. After a time we released the circle with smiles all around. The night felt like a party.

"The chord you have plucked is vibrating," Arrow smiled. "It is already pulling you, us, forward. Let us discuss how that picture might look again."

I had given this question much thought in the past month. It was difficult to hold an image of planetary destiny, and I was pondering whether there might be specific keys to serve as a trigger. A thought had been gathering momentum.

"A place where whales and dolphins do not swim in poison, and we can drink the waters flowing on land. Planetary health will be an indicator of a change in human consciousness," I said immediately.

"Excellent."

"People will see beyond the little dramas of their families, cease inflicting them on the world, and instead recognize their celestial parents," said Victoria. I wondered whether she had had training similar to my own.

"People will treat each other as brother and sister, not as potential enemies," said the African woman.

"Where there is no difference between the inner and the outer," said the Chinese man.

"Can you tell us more?" asked Arrow.

"Where intent is not separated from action."

"More."

"Where intent is informed by Truth, or Source, and forms the basis for the flow of right action."

"Ah!" exclaimed Arrow. "Perfect! Let us join hands and share these visions." He was happier than I had ever seen him.

We connected the circle and felt the energy rising cleanly and effortlessly. Each of us contributed visualizations. I saw myself leaning to drink from a mountain stream that crossed my path, tasting the cool, sweet water. I saw the Amazonian's vision of pure, rich air. As the energy continued to rise we touched the deeper strata of all human action. This layer was informed by connection to Source. Its sustained activation allowed us to join the community of sentient planets. When we could no longer maintain the high level of energy, we dropped hands.

"Those of you who do fire ceremonies, make an offering, not to release the vision but to invite it in," said Arrow.

The mood was festive. Each of us made eye contact with the others, feeling strong connections.

"Let us sing!" exclaimed Arrow. "Sing to the stars, to the planets, to Earth and all her citizens, to each other!"

We sang to all those and more, sending the joy of our vision. As we sang, Arrow did something to the fire that made it look like a crystal with planes, angles, and refracted light constantly shifting. Then he reached in and pulled out a fire seed for each of us, standing to put one in each person's crown chakra. After me, he stepped slightly past and gifted Red Feather before continuing around the circle. Though I didn't sense anything change, Red Feather later told me it was a gift to sustain our vision.

Returning to his seat, Arrow rejoined our song and nodded when we finally fell silent. Then, nodding more forcefully as if responding to an unseen prompter, he said, "Your vision will pull you forward. The logic of love will make the logic of fear and fear-based systems seem ridiculous. The acquisition of power and wealth will seem pointless compared to the joys of Spirit, self-discovery, and connection with each other and the citizens of the Universe. As you hold this vision it will transform your own action toward that which is based in love logic—and it will affect those around you like a ripple or a thought moving through water." He looked at us carefully.

"People say time is speeding up. That is silly, for many reasons, but there is a quickening, an intensification. It is bringing much that was hidden in darkness to the surface. It is necessary. Remember this as the days seem to grow darker." He stopped to gaze at the crystalline fire and then resumed abruptly. "But even so, who wouldn't want to be able to say, 'I was there,' which is why there are so many souls here now. It is not a test exactly, nor is it a spectator sport. Yet it is both. Perhaps it is more like a stadium filled with people, each one of whom is also a competitor. None competes with the other, though quite a few think they do. In reality, each seeks to meet the mark he set for himself before birth. Many may not meet that mark, some because they set it too high and some because they are not ready. There will be other opportunities, and of our times they can say, 'I was there.'"

Had he spoken at such length before? Perhaps I had gotten better at hearing him. We sat silently. Then we reconnected our circle and allowed the energy to rise. It was strong. In an instant the cave was bathed in indigo and purple light. There was a rushing sound. Looking inward I saw the same light surrounding Earth, bringing clarity and wisdom to the beings embodied there. The light changed to white and we began to laugh. All separation and the very important meanings we derived from it seemed to dissolve. The separation was a joke, perhaps the funniest joke in the universe.

The energy level quickly grew difficult for us to sustain. We let it subside and released hands for the final time that night. The doorway opened and people left quickly. Soon only Arrow, Paqo, Red Feather, and I remained seated in our spots.

I wanted to ask Arrow about remembering. It bothered me that when I happened to meet Alfred two months back he had no knowledge about the Council meetings. His response planted a bit of doubt. I posed the question.

"It is what it is," Arrow stated without looking at me. Then he turned and said, "It is very important that you finish your book. I have told you it will have thirty-six chapters. It is a vital part of this vision. You will get what you need."

I saw that Paqo was waiting for me. We stepped into the air outside the cave and then shot off to Ausangate, the great mountain in southern Peru from which so many shamans draw sustenance. It was a wonderful gift from him, yet as we stood on the night summit I realized that either it wasn't my source mountain or I was more tired than I thought. I wondered whether we should try Veronica instead, a nearby mountain I had only seen from a distance two years before but whose black and purple and white form lingered powerfully in my memory. Reading my thoughts Paqo took me there too. At that point I knew I was just unable to run much more energy. I thanked him and left for our starting point.

Standing at the fire circle in my valley I felt somewhat refreshed and suggested to Red Feather that we linger."We could, but your legs are asleep."

True. They were insensate almost to my hips. We rose slowly to the outer world, and I opened my eyes. A window was open and I found I was very cold.

Two hours had passed.

18

The Great Song

~October~
New Moon Entering Scorpio

A month filled with mundane activity passed. I continued to hold the vision from the previous Council session, energizing it in my medicine bundle whenever I could. Life seemed uneventful, at least by my definition, yet I sensed something large slowly gathering momentum.

"The new moon is in Scorpio, my birth moon," I said to Red Feather.

"Mine too."

His reply raised all kinds of intriguing questions that I hoped to investigate later.

When we passed through the door, we greeted a beautiful autumn morning, not unlike the one outside my window. Aquila led us through pines and golden aspens to the usual place.

He had been much in my outer world the past week during a hunting trip. In previous years I found him to be a superb helper for that sort of thing if I opened to his presence and listened to what he was telling me. I had come to rely on him to point me toward our quarry — quail and partridge in the high, brown hills — hearing him say "this way," "here yesterday," or "two remain" after a covey flushed out of range. He helped me to sample the air, noting nuances and direction, and attuning to the small sounds around us. This year our connection extended to locating downed birds in the sage when even the obsessive retrievers had given up. My father and brother were mystified by my apparent dumb luck and spent some time coming up with reasons that to me seemed more improbable than the truth. I let them talk while I thanked the bird spirits and Aquila.

As for Red Feather, he always enjoyed anything that took us out to nature, especially away from the computer, though he wasn't sure about what he called "your ways of hunting." One occasion the year before, I crested a small hill with the wind very much in my favor and saw seven or eight deer playing directly below me. I lowered slowly into the tall grass to watch and heard him shouting, "Shoot! Shoot!" I don't think he understood at all my explanations that this wasn't our prey or that birdshot would have been ineffective.

On the final day of the hunt this year, Aquila simply was not there. Thus I was pleased to see him now and thanked him again for his assistance. I asked where he had been.

"You didn't need me," he responded. "The hunt was over."

In fact it had been a strange day. At the time, I felt a strong pull to be on the road, though I spent the day in the field as planned.

Red Feather, the protector, and I traveled to the boulder field far below the Crystal Cave. In contrast to the bright day where we started, heavy fog clung to the rocks. Visibility extended only a few yards in any direction. We waited briefly before rising slowly in the thickness until level with the cave mouth and darting in. Five Council members were there, sitting in the unlit space. Aside from Arrow, there was Victoria, the African man to her right, Alfred, and Alice. They nodded, but we exchanged no words. I resolved again to learn more about the woman on Arrow's right.

Others arrived closely behind me. Soon our circle was complete. The cave mouth closed and in the moments before Arrow set his magical fire we were in darkness. Green flames erupted. Beginning on his right. Arrow peered carefully into the eyes of each person with a steady, curious gaze. When he reached me, I felt that he was not searching as much as opening to something he hoped to find. He finally turned to the center with slight smile came to his face. The fire became a red globe and expanded, engulfing the cavern.

"It is a healing for you," he said to no one in particular. We had not joined hands, but I felt our connection. As he spoke the light began to shift softly and slowly to orange, then yellow, and on through the visible spectrum until it reached white. With each color I felt my body and energetic field informed in specific ways, enlightening me and bringing me into its resonance and harmony. The white light lingered longer than the rest then shifted down through the colors to red, where it resolved itself as both a singularity in the center of the circle and the globe that still surrounded us. I felt refreshed.

"Join hands," Arrow directed. "Let us energize our vision."

We returned to the vision we had held during the last meeting, the vision of all humankind connected to Source, aware of its own origin and eternal nature. Ten thousand intermediate causes of disharmony and suffering fell away, enabling humanity to recognize the divine within all and to derive sustenance and joy from that knowing. The red globe shifted directly to white, expanding to engulf the planet, the solar system, and then beyond. I sensed that we had reached the limit of our capabilities, for the globe quickly returned more strongly to surround the Earth alone. Yet it was as if we had announced our imminent arrival to the great family of stars and planets. I found we were not even holding hands while the vision of our planet, connected and harmonized within the fabric of the universes, flowed through us like a great song. We looked around the circle at each other as the vision sustained itself effortlessly.

"Your lives are changing. Wonderful things are happening to you and around you," Arrow said after a while. "See each other's stories!"

I looked up at the African man and saw the fruition of a water project he had labored to establish for his town. He had located and activated a new thread of possibility beyond indifference and impenetrable bureaucracy. It was truly an act of personal power with benefit for all, done artfully. With Alice I saw a healing breakthrough with a client that opened an entire vista of possibility for her work. In each, I saw new understandings that enabled things to flow more easily toward positive outcomes well beyond the personal.

"And it will continue to flow," said Arrow, voicing our common realization. "But again, do not make the mistake of saying 'I.' Doing so will diminish your work. If you believe that this power comes only from yourself, it will soon leave you exhausted, and you will die."

There was nothing more to be said. A white light remained around the Earth, almost without any effort on our part, though we could feel the sustaining energy moving through us. After awhile we all left the cave to hang in the air before it. The mist was moving down the valley, and the sun shone on the mounded and shifting fog below. Above us the sky was clear. A question also hung in the air.

"As I told you, for the most part we have moved beyond their ability to comprehend our motives, or their ability to track us," said Arrow, referring to the earlier efforts by unknown persons to hinder our work. "Plus, your own vibrations are higher, which means your defenses are also stronger." He seemed exultant.

How might we appear to someone below? A group of people floating like balloons? Would that person see anything at all? I wanted to be alone with the vast sensations I was experiencing and soon moved off to the top of the crystal mountain. Looking far out to sea, past the diminishing fog bank, I saw a small freighter moving slowly up the coast.

Everything was perfect.

19

Horse Captive

~October~
Second-Quarter Moon in Aquarius

Aquila told me the Traveler was back, though it wasn't a new moon. We went to meet him. He said he would wait three days but no more. I agreed to return within that time and went off to other business. But I forgot my promise until I came to the inner world two days later. Only when I opened the door did I remember. What I had planned for my trip there would wait.

It was a cold, mid-autumn night. The waxing moon hung in the west where the mountains were black against the sky. Aquila and I made our way through the forest to the Traveler's little fire. He seemed unperturbed—perhaps my absence had only been a few moments for him—but he immediately asked, "Where is your friend?" meaning Red Feather. I took a few moments to return to the outer world to retrieve him. And then we three were off.

I heard a furious wind and saw nothing but white. Perhaps it was best to let forms resolve themselves as they often did, but then I found we really were in a blizzard. Was it on a mountain? When the curtain of wind and driving snow parted briefly, I saw we were outside a yurt on the vast central Asian steppe. Not a mountain in sight. A few bony horses stood nearby with their rumps to the gale. Our coming seemed part of this great storm.

We passed inside the tent, not bothering with the entryway and saw a man lying on a low platform to one side. Several others sat nearby in sleepy vigil. They seemed vaguely aware of our presence or perhaps their nodding was only fatigue. A reluctant fire burned in the center as the wind moaned over the smoke hole. Several battered and blackened candle lanterns lit the thick air. The man on the platform was close to death.

I considered the Traveler's predilection for bringing us to places inhabited by northern nomads, usually ones who seemed to be in a bad way. But it occurred to me that perhaps these were peoples for whom the sort of work I did would not seem particularly unusual. Also, the Traveler himself seemed to have a connection.

I returned to the man. What was wrong with him? Sorcery? There were strands of darkness around him. I felt vastly unprepared. Why did I always have to figure it out myself? The life force had already begun withdrawing from his lowest energy centers, but the one in his solar plexus, the center of will and manifestation, was where the affliction centered. On an energetic level that one looked like a bomb crater. Now I felt even more helpless and asked Spirit for assistance. Nothing overt happened, but I recalled how it is said that a shaman is one who journeys to find lost souls. I never really thought of it in those terms, but I softened my focus to see his energy more clearly.

No one was home. His entire soul, not just a piece of it, was gone. Where?

I opened to the possibility of some kind of trail I might follow and found myself ascending through the world of the stone people, past the world of the plant spirits, to the world of the animals where dwell the great souls of all non-individuated Earth creatures, living, extinct, and yet to come. This was why the Traveler had brought me here. Not due to a special skill but because there was something to be learned and because these people had asked for help.

Recently I had worked with bringing people through the stone world or the plant world for cleansing and to balance certain relationships with the spirits of those realms. I had been taught that these are places where one can look for souls of the departed who have passed on without fully cleansing their energetic bodies. But it seemed to me that there must be situations where the living could also benefit from a visit to these realms. I had also learned how to journey to the Lower World in search of lost soul parts, as I did for Red Feather, but not the Upper World. The thought eventually brought me into exactly such situations. And as I had wondered what it would be like to do a healing involving the world of the animal archetypes, here I was.

We were on a great, yellow plain. There was a thunder and horses surrounded me in dust and movement. I sensed deep anger but knew it wasn't directed at me and remained where I stood. Something was very unbalanced. And then I saw the dying man from the yurt on the back of a stocky gray horse of the type ridden by central Asian peoples. The horse was master of the situation, with the man unable to control it or dismount. It was the purest of nightmares, and he was enveloped in an oblivion of terror outside of time.

Approaching one of the moving horses with humility, I asked why they held this man's soul. He bore down on me and stopped at the last instant snorting and tossing his head. I was given a picture of an angry, angry man showing no mercy to the horses that sustained him, beating them cruelly and seizing every opportunity to drive them well past endurance. I heard, "We captured his soul while he was dreaming."

The horses stopped in a circle around me, with the rider clinging blindly to the neck of his unforgiving mount, still seeing nothing but an endless career. What I had heard of his people was that they practically worshipped their horses and the life these animals enabled. What was his story? Raising the question allowed me to tap into something deeper. I saw a boy witness his brother's demise in a gruesome riding accident. The explanations he received for this apparently pointless death made little sense but served to promote a deep enmity toward all animals, especially horses. He grew up to be a hard man whose highest truth was cruelty.

"Will you let me speak to him?" I asked. There was a great stamping and snorting, but they said nothing and remained where they were. I approached the man carefully.

"Wake up! The horses hold your soul!"

He raised his eyes slowly and seemed to come a little out of his fog. Within him I saw nothing but his pain and how he inflicted it on others. The whisper of judgment vanished.

"Your body is dying and you will remain a long time here. I can do little for you unless you decide that you wish to live. If you choose to live, then you must make an agreement with these horses. Then, if your intent is pure, they might release you. What do you say?"

He nodded slowly.

I looked around toward the other horses that had moved much closer. I heard, "Treat us well. Honor us and we will honor you. Your herd will increase beyond the few scrawny nags you now own, and you will know prosperity."

I turned toward the man. "Before you consider their terms, you must release your brother's memory. You dishonor him." We looked into each other's eyes.

Finally, he nodded his head and spoke. "I will do so. I see that it has not served him or me, and there is much I would like to change." Carefully he raised his eyes from mine to his captors. "I ask you horses to accept my deep apology. I promise to live by your terms, if you allow me."

There was silence. At last I heard, "Agreed."

The man sat up straight on the horse that still carried him, looking more like a seasoned rider. Then he swung one leg over its back and came to the ground. He staggered slightly and began to slump. Red Feather, who had been present through all this, moved to the man's left arm while I supported his right. I expressed thanks to the horses and we began our journey down to the Middle World.

In the yurt I found that the Traveler had never left. He smiled innocently at us while we gently laid the soul into the dying body. The man took a sudden, deep breath, then another, activating his form and drawing life force back in. I noticed his solar center, tattered and hollow from the frequent outpourings of anger, begin to soften slightly and fill with light but left it to the healers who were present to finish the job.

"One learns something new every day," remarked the Traveler.

We went out into the blizzard, which seemed to be tapering somewhat, and then back to our meeting place. I thanked him.

"I will return soon," he said, and was gone.

Red Feather seemed fascinated by what he had seen, particularly the horses. But he only said, "They spend much time with those large animals. I could never have imagined such a thing."

I wanted very much to connect with my guide, both because of what had just happened and in order to discuss something from the previous day.

Amun was waiting but only said, "Well done."

We then proceeded to the work I intended before my Mongolian detour. At the end, he asked once again, nodding in Red Feather's direction, "When will you introduce him to his guide?"

20

Things Have Proceeded Faster....

-November-
New Moon in Scorpio

My wife and I were participating in a training to present healing and spirit rites. They were for interested people who were unlikely to undertake the lengthy instruction in our particular pathway. The rites reduced the old rituals of passage to their energetic essence and would be available to any who sought them. In addition there were some rites that were new to us all. A new energy was now coming into the Earth. The training involved giving and receiving several of the rites a number of times each day. In retrospect, the work was synchronous with the unfolding of other events.

The constant jolts and flows of energy strained Red Feather and were draining even for the embodied. He held on without complaint but became increasingly remote. I knew that it was simply his way of protecting himself. On this new moon night we were all tired. I thought of Arrow's statement almost a year earlier that the Council work would be both blessing and burden. Tonight it was definitely burden. A glass of wine and early bed sounded better than a late-night journey for the future of the planet. But Red Feather seemed suddenly present, energized, and eager to do something other than watch me play with live wires.

"Tonight we will journey," he said several times.

We made our way to my valley. A crust of snow lay beneath our feet. The sky was dark but clear. Pausing as always on the valley rim, I could see the Traveler's fire. I was glad. A few days earlier, he returned as promised and made an offer.

"You are strong but unfocused. If you are willing, I will serve as a mentor."

The offer interested me, but I did not respond immediately.

Knowing my thoughts, he said, "Ask your guide. I will wait."

When I asked Amun if this was a good idea, he smiled one of his rare smiles. "I would."

The days that followed were fully engaged with more rites training, leaving little time for anything other than brief meals and sleep. Still, I did make a decision regarding the Traveler.

I greeted him now and said, "I accept your offer on condition that Red Feather be allowed to join us."

"Agreed," he said with a slight smile.

"Can you tell me a little more about yourself?" I asked. "Where do you come from?" This might be a good chance to learn more about him. The Traveler dressed like a Siberian herder or hunter, but he was taller and more European looking. What little hair I could see from under his wolf hat was dark. Wherever he came from, it was cold.

"I am from what you call the future, but it might be better to say that I come through a thin spot. Come. Bring your protector too."

My questions were no closer to being answered.

The four of us traveled to the rocks somewhat farther from the foot of the great cliff face. The Traveler's admonition put me on guard, so I was unsurprised when looking up from our place of relative concealment among the boulders I saw, or felt, two watchers moving near the cave mouth even though it was night. Somehow they stood out clearly, "looking" like symmetrical shadows about ten feet in height, rather boat-shaped with the bow at the top and the blunt end at the bottom. Focusing on them for any length of time seemed to attract their attention. Periodically they swept the area, once or twice passing closely overhead. We waited for hours in invisibility, eyes downcast, thinking no thoughts and drawing on other resources.

Fog crept up the valley, piling against the valley walls. After it had thoroughly blanketed everything, Red Feather and I rose very slowly through the mist and into the cave. Arrow and two others sat in the damp darkness. Members began to arrive singly and carefully but without fear.

When all were assembled, the cave mouth darkened and our fire sprang to life. We joined hands wordlessly, harmonized, and energized our most recent vision. I noticed again how easy it was to re-engage an image from a previous session — the feel and the energy — though it had seemed at the limit of our capacity before. Perhaps it was because we had all held the image and worked with it in the intervening month, or it might have been that simply engaging the possibility was enough to activate it.

As we released each other's hands, two men burst through the doorway as though stumbling through a flimsy wall. They blinked, startled by the firelight, looked around, and then passed within the circle, taking seats across the fire from Arrow. For his part, Arrow only nodded slightly in greeting and then dropped his gaze to the cave floor before him. Like the Traveler, the men were dressed in hide and skins, but they were shorter, more stocky, and darker. They threw back hoods and held their hands to the fire as though admiring its construction rather than seeking warmth. One continued gazing at the fire; the other raised his eyes to the group.

"We heard of this Council and wished to find it for ourselves. It is good to know it exists."

I sensed deep time, as though they came from an ancient age of ice. Their sudden appearance also confirmed the difference between good intent and harmful in enabling unexpected visitors to enter our cave.

We joined hands again, holding our planetary vision and feeling the rising vibration. The visitors put their hands in their laps and engaged our vision too, though after a time I noticed they were less focused on the work and more on Red Feather, whom they seemed to have suddenly noticed. I felt Red Feather acknowledge their curiosity. When we broke the circle again, they rose, nodding to themselves as if confirming what they had seen, and disappeared through the dark curtain at the cave mouth.

Arrow continued as if nothing had happened, gazing steadily into the smokeless fire. Then he raised his eyes abruptly to take us all in with a quick turn of the head.

"Things have proceeded faster than anticipated. We have reached another part of our effort. That work is to connect with our galactic family. How shall we begin? We will start with the Sun, our life-giver, our sustainer. Who can walk this planet and not feel the constant, unchanging love of our Sun for the Earth? It is the greatest love story there is!" Smiling at the thought, he fell silent, then went on.

"There are pathways or cords of energy between us, but they are mostly dormant from disuse. We will energize three that are still active." He sent a picture to us.

I recognized the terrestrial connection points: Mount Shasta, Mauna Kea, and Machu Picchu. I felt part of me say, 'Oh, please.' They seemed to fit current popular mythology so well, and three—all in the western hemisphere—hardly seemed sufficient.

Joining hands we focused on the idea. I could indeed see the connections, faint but steady, between those points and the Sun. The energy went both ways: love from the Sun, gratitude from the Earth. As the intensity of our vibration rose, the three paths thickened from threads to cords and then to great conduits. There was a flash and then another. Lines across the planet sprang to life like acupuncture meridians on the human body. Along those lines, points and high places everywhere emitted or activated their own pathways of energy to the Sun. I saw those paths had also been present and that our little push was enough to animate an entire system. It was a magnificent thing. After a long time gazing at this spectacular sight, I realized we were not even holding hands.

Arrow spoke. "These paths will enable us to energize the next changes. Such changes cannot be done from here alone anymore. The input will also bring darkness into ever more relief—even stimulate it—but because it is fear based it cannot withstand the rising vibration."

I suddenly noted that our crystal mountain itself was activated with an energy line from the Sun and connected to the great planetary web. The entire cave was suffused with a delicate white glow and the crystal behind Arrow was even brighter. We were floating in light. The effect for our cavern and for the Earth itself was similar to working in a room that has gradually darkened; someone enters and turns on a light, asking, why are you sitting in the dark?

"This planet is one of the densest in the galaxy—if not beyond," said Arrow. "A few others are even more dense, but only a couple. Have you ever wondered why we sit near the edge of the galaxy?" He grinned and then answered his own question. "Because at this density everything would fry if we were closer to the center. It's an interesting place, though," he added reflectively. "All who are here have chosen to be here. It offers a good opportunity for accelerated growth and learning." He let us absorb his words.

"Now it is time for us to re-establish our family connections," he said finally. "The Sun itself acts as a buffer between us and the Central Sun. It draws energy from there and gifts us and the other planets a small portion. A direct connection would be too intense, and even what we now get can be too much if we are incautious. It is a gift of pure love. At our next meeting we will energize human hearts from this connection. Those who wish to receive this ongoing transmission—and there are many—will be able to draw on it to effect the great changes that need to unfold and to navigate those changes as well."

The work of the new moon was complete for now. We sat once more in awe and wonder. As the sensation slowly faded, someone asked a question.

"What about the watchers?"

"*They* don't want us to succeed."

"Who are *they*?"

"Those who prefer the way of the last five hundred or thousand years. Probably longer. Luckily in this time ones with skills for such purposes and the intent to use them are few. You have seen how our work has passed beyond the understanding of many who sought to impede us. Still, some remain. Now they are confused about how to proceed, and certain organizations."

I did not know whether Arrow meant there were organizations contributing to *their* confusion or if *they* came from certain organizations. He didn't elaborate.

"Some of this occurs in dreamtime for them, which is also harder to use for such purposes than for ours. Soon we won't be able to hide from them at all, but they will also find it even harder to interfere. They are unsure where to focus and what will have the most effect. Even now they are more annoyance than danger. Yet do not make the mistake of casting these things in terms of good and evil, you only empower their efforts. And I do caution you: continue to take them seriously."

Our luminous crystal mountain seemed to be dimming. The cave mouth opened and Council members began to leave in leisurely fashion. I turned to Arrow, full of questions as usual.

"Why don't people know they participate in this Council?" I asked again. The question continued to bother me.

"Most have chosen to do so in dreamtime," he replied patiently. However, in your case it is important to be awake to record our efforts as accurately as possible." He seemed in a forthcoming mood.

I pressed the opportunity a little.

"What about my friend Red Feather?" I continued to have many questions about him. Amun's answers, when I asked, were reassuring but always vague.

"He has made a great act to be here and to walk this road with you," Arrow said smiling at my thoughts.

The others were gone now. It was time for us to do the same. Did Arrow spend all his time here? The fog was still up. We slipped slowly into it, staying near its top as we drifted seaward. The protector joined us almost immediately. As we came to the beach we dropped straight down into the sand, becoming one of a billion singing voices. I never knew sand could sing, but why not?

The Traveler was at his fire on our return. Looking up, he said, "We begin soon."

21

Red Feather Meets His Guide

~December~
Last-Quarter Moon in Libra

I felt the burden of an unmet promise. Amun asked again. Even my wife asked several times. Yet there were always other things to be done in the inner world. The question of introducing Red Feather to his guide seemed secondary to whatever was "up" at the moment. And something was always up. Of course Red Feather never asked, saying only, "When you are ready." When unmet promise became unfinished business, I knew I needed to make the time.

"How would I go about this?" I asked Amun. I had journeyed to meet my guide for so long it was habit, but I had only recently begun introducing other people to their guides. Results were mixed. Some people hooked right up; others never seemed to get anywhere at all or latched tenaciously onto false guides or archetypal energies. The thought of introducing Red Feather, a disembodied spirit, to his guide seemed even more daunting. Would we journey in his inner world or mine?

"His, of course," said Amun in answer to my unvoiced question. "I will help."

I declared my intent to Red Feather a day beforehand.

"I look forward to it," he said, though I couldn't quite determine his emotion.

Next day, I sat with Red Feather and asked Spirit to help and to protect us both, with a view toward the highest good. I asked Red Feather to picture a cave or an opening in the Earth — a place he knew, or had known. He was familiar with my own journeying and quickly placed us in an ice cave. I was surprised.

"It is a place I went," he said.

We were surrounded by turquoise light, which gave way to indigo as we moved away from the opening down the high, narrow passageway. The way suddenly plunged steeply into deep and ancient cold, a pocket of winter that had forgotten spring. It leveled out again and at length we came to a large pool of blue-green water, perhaps only a few degrees above freezing. At the far end there was nothing but a dim wall of ice. We were at the lowest and final point of the passage.

"I never got past here," said Red Feather.

Did he refer to his embodied form or some other time? Possibly both. A thing I learned during the journey process is that when a path seems blocked it is possible to find or create an alternative. Of course sometimes I went directly to a place when it was already familiar. But for the most part I found there was always something to be gained from the slower approach. Things could change unexpectedly, and being alert to them helped improve my tracking skills.

"We could picture a narrow ledge around the left side," I suggested, "with a continuation of the passage beyond."

We looked again, more carefully. There was a lip of ice skirting the pool and a dark opening on the opposite side above the water level. The lip was enough for us edge the pool with our backs to the ice and continue downward. I was relieved that the entire experience seemed to be Red Feather's and that I could turn my energy more toward assisting him than holding the vision. At least he understood why we had to do it like this for a first meeting.

The way now grew steeper again, and much darker. Red Feather stopped and turned to me.

"I am scared." His admission took a lot of courage.

I realized why he had never pressed me to meet his guide. Without a body to return to—at least in the immediate sense—there was little to differentiate this vision from the world of thought forms that must have continually surrounded him. I recalled the words of the shaman who had brought him into conscious connection with me: "He was living in a nightmare." Since then, Red Feather had been content to accompany me on my own journeys, grounded in my daily life—at least somewhat. Now he was leading.

"I will not leave you," I replied.

We continued, now in total darkness, though somehow it was still possible for us to see. I noticed that the walls of our corridor were no longer ice but rock. Finally there was a widening on the left and a short passage of ten paces ending at a door. The main passage continued down and to the right. The left passage was what I had been hoping for. Although we could have created one as a last resort, it was much better to find one in place.

We turned toward the door. It was T-shaped, in classic Casas Grandes style. Red Feather seemed cheered by the sight. His homeland was in the north, but he had spent a number of years among the ancient Puebloan peoples seeking knowledge, possibly even this moment. There was a flap of tanned hide covering the entrance, decorated with symbols and figures. As we watched, they moved. Red Feather looked at them closely, then at me.

"You first," I said.

We pushed in. I was very curious to see what his sacred garden might look like. At the same time I wanted to keep any pictures and expectations to myself. This was Red Feather's place. Yet I was not surprised. We were in the Yellowstone, or someplace very similar. A set of low, rolling hills was immediately before us. A river wound between the hills, and mountains rose singly in the near distance. Decayed snow lingered here and there, fast becoming standing water. The sky was bright but slightly overcast. I looked around to see whether I could locate the sun but got no hint. That would be someone else's job.

It was Red Feather's turn to be relieved. He had completed the first and hardest step in the process. Now we needed to find a power animal. We pressed straight ahead across the open space until we came to a lone tree that was still leafless but full of buds awaiting the first warm day. A flicker sat there. What else? Red Feather sensed my amusement but immediately began speaking up to the bird in a series of whistles and clicks. He had seen me talk to Aquila often enough in my own work that he knew the question: will you take me to my guide? The flicker turned its head, regarding us with one eye, then took flight to our right, straight over the open fields.

"You will have to teach me that sometime," I said to Red Feather. I had no idea he could do such a thing.

We followed the line taken by the flicker, who would land on the ground, wait for us to catch up, then burst ahead again.

Occasionally we heard his call. A male figure became visible in the distance. The flicker made straight for him, alighting nearby. As we approached, the figure raised his right hand in greeting. Red Feather quickened his pace and then grasped the man's left hand in delight.

"Black Hawk!"

He was a young man of about twenty-five, medium height, copper skinned, with dark hair falling to his shoulders in two braids bound toward the ends by strips of gray fur. He wore no shirt, but his leggings were well made of white buckskin. A fine horn bow hung over one shoulder, and a quiver of nicely fletched arrows was at his back.

"Hello, my friend," he said to Red Feather.

All during our time in this sacred place I noted how much easier it was for me to see Red Feather. Typically I was aware of his form and presence but because he always walked on my left and about a half step back I never got a strong visual picture. Now I noted how closely these two resembled each other. Red Feather turned to me.

"This is a friend from my youth. We called him Black Hawk because there was always a hawk flying near him. We could always tell when he was about to show up." He faced Black Hawk again and the two burst into laughter as if it was the funniest joke ever told. After that they said nothing more but held their gaze while gripping each other by the forearms.

I was moved but also concerned. This could not be his guide. I was certain of it. My own first guide was likewise a close friend in a past life. Yet as far as I knew this was still a continuation of Red Feather's most recent or even his current life. Deceased family members and friends will not be one's guide. Nor for that matter will one's first guide be female. There are a number of reasons for this, and it is also a useful means of distinguishing guides from archetypal energies, or what might also be called gods.

There is more to be said about guides and the archetypes. For now, know that archetypes are powerful forces of living energy, existing well beyond the term that is so loosely applied these days yet permeating our lives at every moment. Brought to consciousness they can work with us for manifestation and healing. Left unconscious within us, or worse, allowed free reign, they make life difficult and incomprehensible. This is the state of many humans on Earth.

I began to look around and was startled to find Amun on my right. He smiled. I didn't trouble myself trying to determine how this was possible. His presence was enough to steady me. Aside from offering counsel when asked, one's guide can help as a transformer for working with archetypal energies. Otherwise, connecting at this level can be overwhelming and possibly dangerous.

Focusing again on Black Hawk I gazed past his left shoulder. Another figure now stood twenty paces beyond, wrapped in an oval of light. I could not determine any features. Red Feather had also noticed the figure and began walking toward it with a steady stride. We followed. As Red Feather approached, the figure began to resolve, becoming a short, robust man with dark brown skin, long black hair knotted at the top of his head, broad nose, and piercing eyes. He had a magnificent jade nose plug and large ear spools but wore a simple red or purple cotton garment that reached his calves. His power was tangible.

"It is his guide," Amun said quietly.

I stepped next to Red Feather. "Ask him if he is your guide," I urged, wanting Red Feather to receive direct confirmation.

"Are you my guide?" asked Red Feather.

"I am."

Red Feather's encounter with Black Hawk had the joy of meeting a long-lost friend. This time, I felt the same surge of emotion from Red Feather that I had experienced on meeting my first guide. It is someone you knew in an ancient life, one who no longer returns to Earth but who is entrusted with your guidance. This person sees you exactly as you are without judgment or blame, never directs or offers opinions unasked, and is always available for assistance. Guides are not guardians, not even to protect you from yourself, but under some circumstances they may offer a warning. Being deeply seen and understood from a place of absolute compassion feels like the home we each seek.

Red Feather fell to his knees. It was a powerful moment. Wordlessly, his guide restored him to his feet. Red Feather looked into his guide's outstretched hands, then into his dark eyes. Another moment passed. The guide turned his head, gazing back over his own right shoulder and raised his hand to point to the sun, which shone brightly. Where had it been before? And then as if creating a path with his hand he brought down the sun archetype, the first and most powerful, to stand before us in human form.

These are all the tests of a true guide to distinguish him from archetypes, spirits, and false guides. Typically it takes a few moments or even a few occasions for an archetype to resolve itself into a meaningful figure, one that draws somewhat on your own inner terrain for form. I was curious to see what Red Feather's Sun archetype would look like but was surprised that it took instant form as a radiant god almost too bright to look upon.

"Ask him what he needs from you to work with you and be your friend," I said to Red Feather.

He repeated the words.

"Allow me to shine through you," the Sun replied.

Red Feather agreed.

"Ask him if he has a symbolic gift for you and if so to place it in or on your body," I said.

Red Feather did so, and the Sun produced a bright disk on a golden cord that he placed around Red Feather's neck, saying, "This will cause you to remember me. It is the power of illumination."

Red Feather's guide grasped his right hand and then grasped the Sun's hand, motioning for Red Feather to complete the circle, harmonizing the energy yet keeping it within Red Feather's tolerance. Both guide and Red Feather began to glow more and more brightly until the guide motioned Red Feather to release the Sun's hand. When the connections were broken the guide bowed his head to the Sun in thanks, motioning Red Feather to do the same. The Sun returned the gesture and with a great rush shot back into the sky.

I prompted Red Feather: "Ask his name."

"I am Smoking Mirror," the guide responded to Red Feather's question. Or perhaps he said Six Smoking Mirror.

Names can be slippery in this realm. I sometimes felt this was where meager ability failed me altogether, but Red Feather nodded. Whatever name he had heard was meaningful. I sensed an ancient connection coming into consciousness. They might have been master and student in some past life, with master invisibly following the student's subsequent lives, helping where possible, allowing the many divergences and errors, and together reviewing things between sojourns.

"Shall we call on the Moon?" asked Smoking Mirror.

Red Feather nodded, overwhelmed but still eager.

Smoking Mirror seemed to do nothing, but another luminous figure appeared before us, resolving almost instantly into a grandmotherly woman in plain buckskin most unlike my own moon archetype. Grandmother Moon! She beckoned Red Feather as if offering him a spoon of soup from a teepee cook pot and he sat before her. She sat too. After a time he asked the same questions as before. Her request was that he always see with his heart, but I could not tell her gift for she placed her hand on the center of his chest. Later he told me it was a green gem. Again, Smoking Mirror, Red Feather, and archetype formed a circle of hands to harmonize the energy. When they had thanked her, she vanished with a pop. It was more than enough for a first encounter.

Smoking Mirror suddenly turned, appraising me in an instant then acknowledging Amun. "I asked Black Hawk to be here to help guide Red Feather to me."

Black Hawk had looked on during the whole series of encounters with a look of undisguised joy. I glanced at him now and received a dazzling smile.

"Red Feather may journey here while you sleep," continued Smoking Mirror. "He knows the way now. He is not dead, at least not like those wandering spirits you help into the Light. He is on a great adventure, part of which is to learn this skill from you. It is an act of supreme courage."

Mixed emotions washed over me: humility, awe, and the desire to be worthy of this honor. I looked at Red Feather, but he simply bowed his head, now completely overcome. It was time to leave.

Red Feather and I rose straight up into the sky and found ourselves slowly passing through rock, then ice. Finally we were at the mouth of the ice cave.

I heard Red Feather say, "I am deeply grateful."

I opened my eyes. The morning had begun dark and gray. Now, a shaft of sunlight fell into the room from an opening in the clouds.

22

The Black Light

~December~
New Moon in Sagittarius
Winter Solstice

I planned to meet Amun. It was morning for me, yet winter twilight was deepening in the sacred valley. Already the brightest stars revealed themselves. I noticed immediately that the Traveler had a fire going and went right to him. As agreed, we had begun to meet at prearranged times for his brand of instruction. His unexpected appearance raised a caution.

Without being specific, he said, "I will guide you when it is time. Remember: stillness."

Stillness had been the first lesson.

I was not planning to join the Council until that evening at the earliest. As usual there was much I wanted to discuss with Amun and much to be done. I acknowledged the Traveler and went on, considering what amounted to a warning.

When to join the Council remained unclear to me. Usually I had a strong sense which day or night around the new moon would be best. Only once or twice had I failed to receive some kind of signal or certainty. Now I knew what that meant. Several times over the next hours, each time I absently considered when to journey, I felt admonition from the Traveler: stillness, invisibility, no thought.

So, we were being watched.

I went about my business as if it was a regular day, which was true, holding a picture in my mind that after dinner I would simply watch some television. Then, when I was ready, I quickly opened sacred space, calling on the four directions, heaven and Earth, and donned a black poncho. I lit a candle in the darkened room, but soon extinguished it. Red Feather and I journeyed in my inner world.

"Sometime it might be possible to journey from mine," he said. I liked the idea.

The night had deepened since my visit in the morning, as if time there had proceeded normally for once. I glanced at the great volcano far off to the right. For the past four years she had blazed like a torch with a continual flow of lava down her sides. I was quite surprised when she first began to erupt, inundating much of my inner world, though not my valley.

"Most people would not have allowed such a remaking. I didn't think you would go that far," Amun remarked at the time.

Actually, I worried that I had not allowed enough.

Things had certainly changed in my outer world since then, but the ever-burning mountain seemed like a constant. Now, in the past few visits, I noticed that the volcano, which had a name, was only smoldering and emitting a dull, red glow. Earlier in the week I asked her about it.

"My work is done for now," she answered. "But you are always welcome to visit for cleansing and to gaze into my fires."

Amun too seemed a little odd, as if withdrawing slightly. I sensed the imminence of more change.

But on this evening I focused on meeting the Traveler. When we stepped into the light of his twig-fed fire, he rose in greeting, then resumed his seat, urging us to do the same while sending the words: no thought. We silenced our minds, or I should say I silenced mine, for I never heard any thoughts Red Feather did not wish to give me. The fire died and the embers cooled. The Traveler finally looked up.

"Now we journey. There will be watchers."

This time we journeyed to one of the pinnacles on the far side of the rocky valley, taking refuge on its boulder-choked summit. The night air was clear and still. I had brought my protector, but his presence began to seem more of a possible attractor and I dismissed him. There were indeed watchers, shadows like him, guarding the cave entrance itself, moving about in the air. One stopped directly before our hiding place then moved off slowly. It seemed that the moment was critical for everyone.

"Mist," said the Traveler, and sent a picture of our bodies becoming thin vapor.

We followed his thought, allowing ourselves to become more and more diffused, atomized, held together only by a memory, such that anyone looking at us would have seen nothing at all. Now this was real invisibility! I felt our vibration increase too and was aware that even though the watchers would have seemed only shadows to anyone seeking them on the material level, we were ghosts to their ghosts. I began to feel that there was very little to keep me there at all and began to drift slowly across the valley, allowing no thoughts. Red Feather did the same, though I was unaware of the Traveler.

We wafted past the two watchers at the cave mouth. I wasn't audacious enough to try moving directly through the voids I could see within them. Inside I found most of the Council present in similar vaporous form, more felt than seen. There was no fire. Three were yet to arrive: Victoria, who sat on Arrow's right, and the gatekeepers, Paqo, and Alice. At last they floated in slowly one by one. When all were present, the cave mouth darkened gently, closing off the starlight. Sitting in the absolute blackness, we came more into form still holding no thought.

Finally Arrow spoke. "To those outside, the cave still seems empty. We are at a vibration beyond their perception." Then, to the unasked question that still seemed to arise, he responded, "They serve ones whose interests are threatened by what we do here. You might be surprised to learn certain identities, but that is not our concern. Directing your thoughts toward them only draws us to their level." He shifted the topic. "Those of you who follow the planets and stars know the significance of these few days. It is the start of the ending before the beginning. Now let us return to our last vision and strengthen it further."

Once again I was amazed that a vision from the previous sitting, attained with some effort, now seemed effortless, merely ground for the next step. A pillar of green fire burst alive at the center of our chamber. Then the whole mountain lit, a crystal node on the great, living web of planetary meridians, connected to the sun. How could the watchers miss this? No matter. The power was overwhelming.

"You are each diamonds," exclaimed Arrow. "You have prepared for this moment, or perhaps it has simply come to you because you are ready. Allow the light to flow through you. Do not attempt to retain it. Otherwise, you will sicken."

I saw light flowing from us to all the other human souls on Earth. Across the globe tiny points began to flare singly or in clusters as something ancient and nearly remembered was activated in those who were receptive. From them the connection continued to others. I felt circles and individuals doing similar work. Arrow said there might be others, and I knew it had to be so. Now they were evident. I recognized we had become a single, thirteen-sided diamond as the light force flowed through us at greater and greater intensity. At a moment I looked around in wonder and found other Council members doing the same. The flow continued unabated.

"In ages past, you would be called prophets," Arrow said. "People would have looked to you for illumination, a religion perhaps. Those days are over. Now it is available to each person to be his own prophet and to find a direct connection to the Light. That is what we have done tonight." He paused. Looking at me out of the corner of his eye, he smiled slightly. "We are the ones we have been waiting for."

I smiled too, for I knew someone else who used this phrase well before the politicians found it.

"We are our own messiahs." He waited for this to sink in. "Not everyone can do what we are doing yet, and there is much resistance that is fed by the intense gravity of the past. But there will be enough to continue the wave. It is now self-sustaining."

I glanced at Red Feather and could see his features in sharp relief from the green pillar of fire and a white light suffusing our crystal mountain. Around the circle, people soaked in the energy.

Then I saw the Black Light. It seemed to be entering my body from my right side. Later I considered that I had been sitting in my room with the west on my right, though not in the cave. Certainly it did not come from above, as the white light seemed to do. Nor was it from the sun. I realized it was coming through the lens of Pluto, then in direct alignment with the center of our galaxy and conjunct the sun, as though filtered through a lens. It was a living black light, living darkness as if from a dark crystal. Was it a lower octave or resonance of the white? No, it didn't seem so. I glanced up to see others looking to Arrow for an explanation.

"Some might call this light evil. It is possible to pervert it, and it has been, but it is essential to Creation. This is the Great Secret. Just as night follows day or yin follows yang. The key to manifestation is the dance of the two. Allow it to enter you, combine it with the white light."

I did so and experienced strange and wonderful sensations and realized I was emanating a dark purple hue. Looking around, I saw some of the others emanating all kinds of beautiful colors.

"Little Feather! Try harder!" Arrow barked at me.

I added intent and got better results, even a little gold and silver. Shortly, the black light began to fade leaving the cave suffused again with gentle white light.

We returned to our individual diamond forms, this time sending light to specific individuals. I found I could see their diamond natures, obscure even to them. Their chakras were in various states of activity or suspension, even occlusion. In the case of one friend, I saw what I had guessed recently: his deceased grandfather was in his body as well. The large, double-terminated crystals I used for extractive purposes supposedly resembled the energetic aspect of the human body. Now I could see the similarity clearly.

I was tired. Some of the others were flagging a little as well.

"I have a surprise," Arrow said quietly.

As we turned toward him, the cave floor suddenly became transparent. We could see all the way down to the living fires of the Earth. It was like looking through clear lake ice, except this was though miles of rock. Everyone gazed in wonder at the beautiful gift, which slowly subsided after a few minutes.

"Keep the diamond vision alive and active," said Arrow, as though handing out a homework assignment at the end of class. "We will work more with the Black Light later. That was just a taste." Continuing in classroom mode, he looked around, open to questions. None forthcoming, he said, "Leave the way you came. Atomize. Drift out like a slight breeze."

I was the first to rise. Red Feather and I slowly became mist and filtered through the dark curtain across the cave mouth. The watchers were still there, vigilant, looking over the valley. I floated left down the valley and out to sea. There was a fog bank several miles offshore, which I slipped into gratefully. This new mode of invisibility—or higher vibration—was hard to sustain. I moved down into the water, deeper and deeper. A pod of whales was cruising north. Thinking of a diamond, I illuminated them. They had crystalline forms as well, yet I could clearly see their eighth chakras above and somewhat in front of them in addition to seven other centers in their bodies. Did I hear one of them say, "Thanks!" as they passed into the darkness?

I drifted through the Earth back to my valley, aware again of Red Feather. The Traveler had not reappeared. Still, we lingered at his cold fire briefly before I returned to my physical body like a vapor. It was a slow process and I was even more tired than in the cave. I sat in the dark, observing the glow of my hands under the black wool of my poncho. It was an interesting effect and certainly not one I had seen before. I was aware that in this sacred space, open until I closed it again, the lineages of each direction were present, sitting in power with quiet joy.

It was almost exactly a year since the Traveler's first appearance.

23

Crystals

-January-
New Moon Entering Aquarius

The next new moon arrived quickly. As each one followed the next, I found myself feeling increasingly unready both physically and energetically. It had taken some time to recover from the intensity of our work at the previous moon. Now I wondered if the recovery was incomplete. I recalled Arrow's words about blessing and burden. Today, burden.

Early morning seemed the best time. Red Feather and I started down. I'd been feeling distant from Spirit, which was unusual for me. Everything seemed stuck. Lately I wondered if something had happened to cut me off. Perhaps there were forces or entities working at this. Perhaps I could just let it go once. Maybe this was the one time we didn't meet. Why couldn't they meet without me?

We paused at the door. I had to continue, but I wanted to try for more focus. It all seemed so difficult suddenly, and rather silly. I turned to Red Feather. Since meeting his guide, he had been very quiet. Now I could see him well, perhaps because he had something to say.

"Before going into battle, a warrior should feel joy," he said.

I hadn't thought of this as battle, but I understood. His words were what I needed. Seizing the door I stepped in. It was dark before dawn, frosty cold. I sought the Traveler's little fire from the valley rim and saw it plainly against the dark. He had been there all week. I thought at first that he had some adventure or errand for me, but he only said, "I will wait. Stillness." I understood and was confident, yet his presence as I came and went also made me apprehensive. These days he didn't appear without good reason.

"Use all the invisibility you can," he said, without rising.

"Should I use a dragon?" I asked. Over the past year and a half I had occasionally worked with that dragon energy: a strange, archaic force that had grown within from a single seed planted during work with another shaman. We had touched the subject in Council recently, and earlier in the week I applied some of that energy with surprising effectiveness. I was rather proud of it.

"No. You have not mastered that yet."

There was something in his tone that I understood only much later. He rose.

We traveled to the mountaintop opposite the crystal mountain. It was sunny, slightly misty. Immediately I saw two things. First, every Council member seemed to have arrived at the same spot simultaneously. Second, across the valley twelve watchers were arranged before the mouth of our cave. Where was Arrow? I could not tell if he was present, for there was no time to count heads. The watchers were arrayed in formation with an energetic web between them. There would be no drifting in this time. Move and countermove. I felt no fear, just irritation. I had seen such webs before. With a quick look at each other, we formed a sort of flying wedge, like a black arrow, and roared straight at the obstacle. Whether by surprise or force, we had little problem blasting through something that offered no more resistance than cobwebs. Looking back from within the cave, I could see the watchers scattered in disarray, confused and powerless to follow.

So much for invisibility.

Arrow was there. Even before we seated ourselves, a green flame burst into life at the center, man-high. He nodded to Alice and the cave mouth darkened.

We joined hands immediately, the crystal mountain lighting up as if continuing exactly where we left things a month ago. We were crystals, double-pointed, radiating the same energy as before to humanity, then to Earth, and then to the solar system and beyond, witnessing all the planets in various states of awareness. It was another awesome sight. I heard Arrow's words, "Listen to the harmony." Indeed, each planet had a series of vibration points that resonated with the others like a great harp of ten thousand strings. Our crystal energy added to the music. Soon, however, it became difficult to sustain our energy over such vastness. We returned the sphere of our efforts to our own planet. I saw her in her energetic form. She seemed to be coming into awareness of her own crystalline nature. It was difficult to stop watching, particularly because our awed gaze seemed to be activating this reality.

Arrow finally broke our mesmerization and brought us back to the cave, which remained bright, the soft light gently pulsating.

"Things are speeding up now. Always use this cave and your experiences as a touchstone and anchor. As I keep telling you, the old, dark ways will not fall away without a struggle. That is to be expected. You have heard a lot of talk about 2012. Twenty-twelve is just a number. The things said to occur on that date and in that year are already happening. Our Earth is giving birth to herself. Births always have the potential for danger and pain, but what are the alternatives?" His soft voice was loud now. "You! You are the midwives. And on the day after some date in 2012, what? Think of a baby. It is not born an adult, and even then, what if it was? On that day there will not be an instant golden age. Life is messy," he smiled, "and your job as midwives and helpers will continue." He allowed us to consider.

"Return to the vision you started with a year ago. We have been to the edge of the solar system. Now let us energize the first vision again."

I tried to remember what my vision had been, but could only come up with a picture of me drinking from a pristine steam in a deep forest, tasting sweet, pure water. If the water were pure enough to drink, then many unbalanced things would have been harmonized. It was still the quickest and best indicator I could envision. From there I saw myself walking in brotherhood with my fellow humans. I thought about a movie clip I had seen earlier in the week. In an interview, one of the Lost Boys of Sudan was puzzling over life in America. "How can it be that you are all Americans, yet you aren't welcome to walk into each other's homes?" he asked. I had laughed out loud at the clash of two cultural logics, yet I could understand his perplexity. Why not?

"We will draw in the Black Light to give it form." Arrow said. "Allow the White Light and the Black Light to mix." We began, but then he added, "Your visions are not so far apart and are shared by many others on Earth."

It is difficult to describe the effect. I felt sensations of deep harmony and balance gathering and joining in me as a crystal being and within our shared energetic field. How would humans walk upon the Earth?

There were no visions of great cities and golden civilizations. Perhaps that time was over or such visions were too limited for a new way of being. I was content to focus on the feelings. We released it as a great, evolving thought form and allowed it to expand outward in all directions.

The sensation of existing in crystal form remained with me. I looked around, making eye contact with each member. It was easy now to see each of them. Everyone was smiling and relaxed, untroubled by what might be outside our cave.

After we had rested in the glow for a short time, Arrow nodded to Alice and Paqo. The curtain across the cave mouth drew back, and we saw twelve watchers trying to peer in. One for each of us? Their web had been re-energized and strengthened, the energetic cords between them glowing dully.

"You should probably leave the way you arrived," Arrow said calmly.

"What about you?" someone asked.

"I have my own means," he replied in the same tone.

Taking his advice, we shot out as a single form into the sunlight. It felt so good that we continued up right into the living heart of the sun. The energy was intense and vital but hardly the vaporizing, million-degree heat one would experience for a tiny instant in bodily form. Rather, it was a living energy, holding us in cool, cleansing force. Our group drifted apart slowly, each finding a separate way home. I was concerned for Red Feather's well-being but relaxed when I felt him smile at the experience. We returned as a dust mote or particle in the solar wind, slowly falling to Earth and back to the fire in my valley. The Traveler was there. Had he been with us the whole time? I wasn't sure.

He looked at us for a moment before exclaiming, "Excellent work!" Then he simply disappeared.

We stayed for other matters. Later, as I gazed from my kitchen window at the Sun rising over the mountains, I suddenly remembered: I had just been there.

And then I recalled something else: I too had a new guide.

24

The Sixth Sun

-February-
New Moon Entering Pisces

I awoke from uneasy dreams. It was time for the next Council meeting, and Arrow's voice sounded in the far distance. Yet I procrastinated, hoping to shake off the residue of dreamtime. Although I journeyed all the time, the work of the Council never seemed to get easier. Half an hour later, I was no more centered than when I opened my eyes. The only thing was to hope the journey itself would have an effect.

At the door it was my turn to pause. I turned to Red Feather.

"I am sorry we have not been to see your guide again. I know it is something you have been wishing for. We will."

Several times I had felt his strong desire for a second meeting, yet there always seemed so much to do just in my own inner world. Among them was the need to integrate my own new guide, an occurrence that was deeply surprising. I knew that Red Feather's guide said they would meet in dreamtime while I slept, but I also knew without asking that they had not met again. Perhaps the way was still unclear for him, or the prospect of becoming unmoored from me was daunting.

"It is not necessary to say so, for I know we will," he responded. "I rely on you to select the moment. Where would I be without you?"

Always an interesting question!

I opened the door and we stepped in. The weather was miserable—a hard, sleeting rain turning to mushy snow—no doubt foretelling conditions in the outer world. We proceeded to the valley rim where I asked the protector to accompany us.

When we met Aquila, the wolf said, "He is not here," meaning the Traveler. I sensed that too, but Aquila led us to the Traveler's place nonetheless. A few days earlier I got an idea to journey directly to the cave, entering through the floor. Why hadn't this occurred to me before? I asked the protector to travel only as far as he could.

Setting the intent, I could feel us passing instantly though earth and rock and then moving up through the crystal mountain itself more slowly. Red Feather and I emerged in the cave. The mouth was sealed and a green fire burned in the center.

"Well done, well done!" Arrow said as soon as we appeared. "I sent you that idea. Your vibration is high enough now that you can enter directly."

I was relieved to avoid the drama at the cave mouth, particularly as I had been puzzling the significance of twelve watchers for twelve Council members. I didn't like any of its possible implications. Others were arriving in the same fashion. As each appeared like rapidly coalescing smoke from the walls or floor, Arrow greeted them with a hearty "Well done!"

"What if one of us had trouble?" I asked.

"Then we would have to go help...him," Arrow replied, turning at the last word to give me a big smile. Some of the Council members laughed.

When all were present we exchanged greetings. I began to move my gaze clockwise around the circle, connecting with each person. It seemed that although I had not met many of them in the flesh we were slowly establishing relationships.

The skin of a jungle cat had come my way, having passed unused through several hands over the years until it reached mine. I was hesitant to accept it at first, until I realized it was meant for me and began working with its spirit. The last owner was happy to be rid of it, stating that it was a jaguar. When I unwrapped the skin from its black cloth, I found it was too small for a jaguar and the spots were different. It was something more like an ocelot, a quick little thing that cut less of a swath than a jaguar. I had felt it following me around the house lately and began calling on it for certain assistance. My dogs took one sniff at the pelt and then kept their distance. My immediate impression was that it came from the Amazonian. Meeting his gaze now, I sought confirmation.

He nodded, smiling, and I heard him say, "In fact, it is from my father. I am glad it has finally found you. He is no longer with us, but he saw that you would make good use of it. He killed it himself with great honoring. It has a strong spirit!"

I returned his nod, sending deep appreciation, and then moved slowly around the circle to the others.

"When are you coming to visit?" the African man asked me.

"When I have some more money."

"Ah, a little more time to manifest it!"

Arrow motioned for us to join hands. As always, we rose quickly to the energetic level of the previous meeting. Once again we were a single gem with thirteen facets, embodying and containing the Earth crystal, bringing light into her, sustaining the vision without effort. At a certain point we felt a sudden sense of release and a great jet of darkness streamed from us into the sun. The ancient injustices, the old wounds, and the fear that festered and was exploited for centuries on centuries moved like an oily river to the sun's flame where it was transmuted. Slowly, the flow diminished to a trickle and then ceased.

"Fill that space!" Arrow shouted.

A stream of light shot back from the sun to the Earth, illuminating and empowering our newly unburdened planet. I do not know whether it was the energy that had just gone into the sun, transformed, or something else, but the feeling was remarkable. Finally, we released hands.

"Thirteen *is* more powerful than one!" Arrow exclaimed as if surprised by the idea.

The Crystal Cave glowed, almost outshining the green fire. We luxuriated in the continuing effects of the release and enlightenment. So many dark things were coming into the light these days.

At last, Arrow spoke. "It is the end of time and the beginning of time. A great cycle comes to a close, another begins—the Sixth Sun!"

I could feel the questions. Many of us had heard of the Fifth Sun or the Fifth World, whose time was supposed to be at hand. Now the Sixth?

"I call it the Sixth because it sounds better in English," he said with a twinkle. "Easier to say, too. Why would it be this way? It is the way of things as expressed in many traditions. Cycles of light alternate with cycles of darkness. There are lessons in both. Do not make the mistake of calling one bad and one good. And," he looked around for emphasis, "it is the way of Spirit, the way Spirit comes to know itself." He waited for us to absorb the meaning.

"What a fine time to be alive!" he continued, allowing us to feel his genuine excitement. "And you have indeed all chosen to be here. You are not from here. You are from far and diverse places. After many lives in human form, here you are at this critical point. Yet you have only been in this world for an instant!

"I know each one of you has stood in great weather storms, marveling at the overwhelming power, perhaps even searching them out when others sought shelter." There were nods and smiles. "Yet you knew they would not last. So it is now. Darkness approaches, but you and many others will be the lights. Stand your ground! Shine!"

"What about the prophecies?" someone asked.

"Prophecy is over. Those warnings have been heeded—by many, and enough. Those visions we have held of a new world? *That* is prophecy now. You are your own prophets. Keep bringing in the two lights—the black and the white—to activate your visions. They will pull you forward into the next great cycle."

We were silent a long time.

"Join hands," Arrow said abruptly. We became one crystal, again bringing in light to the living and emerging Earth crystal, helping her manifest changes in her structure. Then we expanded to include the entire orbit of Earth around the sun, enfolding the inner planets and the star itself. From there we expanded to include the full solar system. I noted several planets in other dimensions, still "undiscovered" yet waiting to be found as human perception expanded. Each shared counsel with the others. I saw how on Earth that energy so often became twisted and filtered. Why was it here particularly that the human inhabitants always seemed to arrive at the right place, finally, by the hardest means?

I felt that our energy was overextended. Our sphere shrank back to the sun alone, itself in process of change but different from Earth. We could feel its pure love, radiating to the other planets, transforming overwhelming energy from another dimension into beneficial emanation. Finally we followed that transformed and transformational energy back to our own planet, lingering in its fire after releasing each other's hands. No one was in a hurry to leave.

I turned to Emeen on my left. We exchanged greetings in Arabic. She saw my questions about her presence in such a shamanic setting. I was embarrassed to be caught in an assumption, but she smiled.

"The beauty of the Prophet's teachings was quickly seized by lawyers and conquerors, yet it still shines for those with eyes to see and hearts to understand." Then she darkened. "May God send light to the souls of those young people who do such horrible things in the name of faith. May our work here open a door for them." She moved her eyes away.

I felt slightly chastened and said nothing more until Arrow turned to me.

"The Traveler has been teaching you some things."

"Yes, though I feel less than apt."

"He looks for people like you and has a few other students."

"Who is he?" I was still no closer to understanding.

"He is of this time but not of this time. Someday that will make sense." He moved to face me fully, completely serious. "Listen, you must publish this book very soon. It is important." Having regarded me for a few moments, he turned to the group, resuming his cheerful attitude.

"Be sure to take some of this home with you." He pointed to the fire, and laughed as if referring to leftovers from a dinner party.

People began to leave the way they had arrived. Red Feather and I journeyed back to my valley and found Aquila where we had left him. The protector also rejoined us. It was still gray and sleeting. I wanted Red Feather to meet my new guide. We passed down the valley, following the general course of the stream, still mostly frozen, and came to the rough stairs I always ascended to meet Amun. A new portal was open at the foot. There stood my new guide, observing Red Feather.

"So, you finally brought him. I am glad!"

Red Feather had already gone to one knee, eyes downcast.

"Thank you, but please stand," said my guide with a slight smile in his great beard.

It was only polite to introduce them, though they probably already knew the other's name.

"Red Feather," I said, "this is Odínn."

25

Odínn and the Inner Guides

Odínn was the fourth of my inner guides. Like most of the others, he appeared suddenly. Each one replaced the previous at junctures that seemed obscure but in retrospect are obvious. Equally obvious from hindsight were indications for change that had been present for months. Only my love and fully-grown connections kept me from seeing the signs or hearing the plain words.

The way of the inner guide itself came to me unsought, at least not consciously. Of course it too was perfectly timed and launched me on a path that diverged increasingly from the one whose course I assumed was permanent. Now I cannot imagine a life without the anchoring presence of a personal guide in my inner world and the ready availability of compassionate, nonjudgmental counsel.

)

One day, idly browsing a bookstore, I reached for a title but another literally fell into my hands. It was *The Inner Guide Meditation*, by Edwin Steinbrecher. Perusing it, I completely forgot my surroundings until my wife finally suggested I buy it so we could leave. Why had I never encountered this book? I read widely in the so-called occult and was in the book business myself. This one offered simple yet powerful steps to connect with a personal guide in one's life. It also gave detailed instructions to begin navigating the inner world in order to work with archetypal energies. The author stated that my guide would be a human male and why. Perhaps the guide would be someone I knew in a previous life but not from this one, someone who might have served in a teaching or guiding role then too. While the author spoke of endless vistas and powerful interactions with the beings and energies one would encounter, he was also explicit in his warning never to venture far in these realms without some kind of trusted guide, offering a cautionary tale from his own early experience.

With great trepidation I made my first journey to a sacred garden. I met a power animal, the wolf Aquila, who then led me to a tall man with a tousled head of dark brown hair and a short beard. He wore the clothes of a medieval monk. When I asked, the man said his name was Dmitri. I subjected him to several tests to verify him as a true guide rather than a false one. He submitted graciously. We began working together, carefully at first, meeting the archetypes of universal energy represented in the major arcana of the tarot one by one. The process was laborious and took the better part of a year. What at first was a ten-minute morning meditation expanded to an hour or more on a near-daily basis.

The word "archetype" is lately and popularly assigned to what one of my subsequent guides once dismissed as "scripts." While those mythic stories have powerful hold on us and are well worth examining, he emphasized that they are primarily cultural constructs or human thought forms. Instead, I came to understand that each archetype is an aspect of living universal energy that exists outside of person or culture, though it informs both levels in specific ways. Moreover, the twenty-two archetypes of the major arcana have planet and zodiac correspondences within one's astrological chart that allow us to bridge the gap between an intellectual appreciation and direct engagement with the operative forces in our lives. I began to suspect that what I considered my identity in this lifetime was essentially the nexus of a unique arrangement of these archetypal energies. The thought was both lonely and liberating.

Much of the work involved bringing all the archetypes into consciousness as luminous figures that slowly resolved into specific appearance. I sought to create harmony among them so they could engage with each other and with me rather than work at cross-purposes. Some were friendly and familiar, some resistant or overbearing, and some were just howling angry. Again and again, I came face to face with my personal projections, all in the process of bringing balance to what at first seemed like a kindergarten of misbehaving gods.

I find now that I can see the gods at work in other people beyond my own projecting—if I have their permission to look. All sorts of life issues can be addressed at a high level in this powerful modality. The distinction between outer and inner, what is real versus what is supposedly imaginary, is merely our worm's-eye view and as useless as the tired idea of a mind-body dichotomy.

Dmitri told me we knew each other from a lifetime when we were both monks—not very good ones by church standards. For one thing, we never skipped a tavern. But we loved God wholeheartedly and went wherever we felt called. He showed me how I died too, during a siege in which I was assisting a town of "heretics." There were other lifetimes as well, all connected in some way with my current life. He said this particular one was a culmination of sorts, for me and for many others here, though he also cautioned me to remember that past and future were simply products of linear time and that all lives exist simultaneously.

Another time I asked him if we were in heaven. He laughed, as he always did, and said, "No, this is Elsewhere. There are many heavens, as real to their inhabitants as your world is to you, but Elsewhere interpenetrates them all." He also explained that it was a place where the archetypes are most active or undiluted.

At a certain point I began to experiment with combining the archetypal energies into composite beings. Many of them seemed to bear the name of ancient angels. Dmitri told me they were the active consciousness of Creation and that there were many thousands of combinations. I thought of the ancient Hebrew lore that mentioned 70,000 angels and the lifetime efforts of quite a few people to catalog them. "More!" he said laughing.

)

This activity seemed to trigger something. After I had been doing it for a while, Dmitri said, "You will be getting a new guide soon." I dismissed the idea as common human desire for promotion and remained content working with a teacher who saw me exactly as I was and who was willing to help me a few steps down an amazing road of discovery. A few months later he said the same thing, adding, "I have gone as far as I can with you." Developing trustworthy inner vision requires vigilance toward one's own thought forms, I reminded myself. Again I rejected his words as the product of prideful thinking. He let it pass.

But a few days later, just after my birthday, there was someone with him. Without my asking, he said, "This is Pentheon. He will be your new guide." Behind Dmitri's shoulder stood a short, kind-looking man with close-cropped white hair and stubbly beard. His dark eyes were alive, and he was dressed in a white robe of coarse cloth. He was barefoot and wore something that looked like a skullcap. I was highly suspicious and ran him through the same tests as I had imposed on Dmitri. He performed them effortlessly.

Then I asked both about a dream from the previous night. Although I addressed Dmitri, he deferred to the newcomer who responded without hesitation. From there we three continued on to some archetype work at a level of energy higher than before. The next day I journeyed to Elsewhere with great expectation, but only Dmitri was there. I was surprised by my own disappointment. The day after that, Dmitri seemed to be alone, but where I looked more closely, Pentheon came into focus, wearing his white wool *jalaba* with the hood thrown back. I was pleased to see him but had to ask Dmitri, "Why wasn't he here yesterday?"

"You were too eager," he replied, as if Pentheon had been there but I wasn't able to see him. It was humbling. Yet being in Pentheon's presence felt wonderful. I noted in my journal that there was a calm but powerful energy about him, as well as strength and artfulness in his approach to the archetypes. My love for Dmitri was undiminished, but within a few days he became almost ghostly and then was gone. When I asked about him, Pentheon said, "He's not here. You can see him whenever you want." I looked again and Dmitri was present, smiling.

"You will be working with him now," Dmitri said, "because your work involves things that I can't help you with. But I will always be here." I could feel his love.

And so Pentheon guided me for the next year. I now see that he gently moved me away from the play-business of creating "angels" toward more direct and authoritative engagement with the archetypal energies, much in his own manner.

We had once shared a life in Etruria, or pre-Roman Tuscany. Soon he showed me how to access a beautiful little wild garden that was his at the time. In one mossy corner water trickled from the mouth of a stone face set in an ancient stone wall. Thereafter we met in its coolness although I continued to enter through my own valley.

I was a young student in that life, promising but headstrong, as he often told me. I saw myself frequently seeking fields and streams to hunt and roam free but mostly to escape the stink and filth of ancient village life. I loved horses and loved riding them. During one of those outings I encountered him at his place and soon entered a sort of apprenticeship with him.

One day he needed me to run an errand. Impetuously I hopped on a big stallion that was somewhat beyond my abilities, against Pentheon's standing instructions, and was off before he knew. The roads there were already ancient, and some were worn deep into soft volcanic rock. Rounding the corner of a close-walled thoroughfare at full gallop I barreled into an oxcart that was wedged sideways. My horse reared, I fell off, and that was the end of that. I also saw my spirit leave my body. It looked around a little, realized what had happened, and turned its attention to an opening that was beginning to coalesce in the air. As the opening became a brilliant tunnel, I could see a welcoming figure just inside. Light poured over the entire scene, unobserved by the gathering knot of passersby, but the spirit was drawn almost magnetically. There was a rushing noise as it moved into the tunnel and was obscured by the brilliance. I felt a wave of pure, nonjudgmental love and the joy of returning to a truer, fuller self. The opening folded in on itself, leaving only an unnaturally posed corpse on the ground, and then was gone.

Pentheon told me occasionally that my passing had been a deep disappointment to him and that it pleased him to serve as my teacher and guide again. I came to love him as much as Dmitri, though the two had very different personalities. For one thing, Pentheon was sterner and more demanding.

"You might fall off another horse," he once said to me.

)

A year later, when winter had begun in Elsewhere, Pentheon said, "It's time for your new guide." It was my exact birthday. I realized he had been serious when he mentioned a new guide once or twice. I had even seen a figure standing a few paces behind him, but I had not tried to hasten the change. For one thing I got the feeling that it would mean more intense inner work. For another, I just didn't want to hear. On this day, the new guide simply took Pentheon's place. His name was Amun, and I recognized him as the welcoming spirit at the mouth of that tunnel of light. I found myself longing for the easy gruffness of Pentheon, but he was just gone.

I knew right away that Amun was a true guide. I ran him through the tests anyway, missing Pentheon deeply, but excited by the change. Amun was strong. His quiet power dwarfed what I had known in Pentheon, though the comparison felt disloyal. Unlike the two earlier guides it took a few days for his image to resolve, something that continued to require occasional effort. A journal entry several days after meeting him reads, "I'm not sure if I had encountered him first off whether I could have handled his power."

And power, real power, formed the basis of his gentle lessons. After all the fireworks of working with the archetypes, experimenting, combining, harmonizing, and retaining them in consciousness, Amun directed me toward a deeper, more essential view. We discussed the nature of intent, love, destiny, and above all the relation of human to Source. He guided me effortlessly for seven years, during which time my life shifted in ways I would never have been bold enough to imagine.

He immediately he showed me our life together. It was in Egypt, long predating the life encounters with the other guides—at least in linear time. I was an ignorant village boy tending a few goats when he came through my muddy existence. This seemed well before the great Pharaonic dynasties, for a far more substantial history extends past the arrogant scope of our present times. I wondered whether he might have been *the* Amun, later known as Amun Ra, the sun god, but he only smiled his gentle smile when I asked. It was of little consequence.

During that lifetime, several other students and I accompanied him up and down the Nile, apparently serving as healers and teachers. Beyond that, our lives and purposes are still unclear to me. I do know that we were welcomed quietly wherever we went and that I died a natural death. Occasionally, after I did something in our current relationship that he appreciated or when I came to a deeper understanding of an issue, he would smile and say, "Pretty good for a goat-boy." We met once at Pentheon's place, and then a new portal opened onto Amun's world of the Nile Valley, where we then continued.

More than a year after my first inner-world meeting with Amun, I was returning from a horse-pack trip into the high mountains. The camping and fishing had been fine, and I was enjoying the scenery on the long trail out. At one point I pondered the Etruscan life with Pentheon, how much I loved to ride then and how much I distrust horses now! I thought perhaps I could call on some of that youth's riding experience. Instead, I fell off my horse when we stopped on a steep and rocky section, the horses all bunched and skittering and the indifferent wranglers telling us not to worry. It was so steep that I had to lean until I almost touched the saddle with my back. The saddle began sliding up over my horse's shoulders, and then I was on the ground. As I laid on the boulder-strewn trail, I turned my head and saw a large, sharp stone, inches away, and realized it could have easily split my skull. Yet I was whole and able to indulge my anger toward the cowboy who had told me not to wait a few moments at the top of the hill. He just laughed when I turned to my wide-eyed horse and said, "It's not your fault." At the same time I was also strangely jubilant. I was alive and something had shifted.

I asked Amun about it as soon as I could. He pointed to that former life with Pentheon and told me that I was now literally picking up where I had left off so long before. The circle was finally closed: an end in one life and a beginning in this one.

"Do not be afraid of the changes that come to you in your life now," he said. "It is part of your next step."

Just a week later I set foot on the shamanic path with intent. It opened a new way of viewing the world, one in which trees, stars, and rocks had things to say to me, and I approached the notion of being a healer — something I never considered before. I dreamed about coins, which Amun told me represented change. He also said it would be my task to integrate the inner-guide work with this equally powerful new way.

"There is no disconnect, but it is your job to find the common aspects and unite them."

A year on, I told Amun that I was having trouble integrating the two approaches.

"No you're not," he replied immediately. "This," he said, meaning the inner guide work, "is the path of the left. The other is the path of the right. It is not a matter of masculine and feminine. Rather the right is more outwardly oriented. It centers on ritual and ceremony whereas this is the more inwardly directed. Just as both hands can do the same work, both paths are valid and effective. But remember also that one hand can often do a particular task better than the other. You can make rain from either side, but the approach will differ. And by the way, you need to practice rainmaking again. You have become adept at the left-hand path. Now you begin on the right-hand way, the one more directly related to the outer world. We are well pleased."

I wasn't sure whom he meant by "we," but I recalled a recent ceremony during which I had received beautiful seed-gifts of power. I clearly saw Amun, Pentheon, and Dmitri standing and smiling at me. And past Amun I saw another, future guide, whose form and visage was indistinct.

)

There came a time when I began to work with the great archetypes in a new way, one that was also more directly connected to the outer world, though not in ceremony. I also found that I could now pass some of the tests that differentiate real and false guides myself. Amun encouraged me and offered specific advice. Looking back, this was also when he began occasionally suggesting I introduce Red Feather to his own guide. I had no inkling that it would mean a new guide for me too.

Soon after Red Feather and I met Smoking Mirror, I journeyed alone to meet Amun as usual. I had in mind a few items of inner business and supposed Amun might add something else, which he often did. Instead there was a great bear of a man standing to his left. I identified him instantly as a guide, though Amun had never mentioned the possibility. I was not keeping a journal at the time, which I now regret, but I remember the meeting and the ones that followed well enough.

Without ceremony Amun said, "This is your new guide. His name is Odínn."

I looked at the new guide and then at Amun.

"I appreciate his presence, but I am pleased with our arrangement."

"He can better help you with the things you are now doing."

The thought of not meeting Amun was almost more than I could bear. I loved his quiet power and mastery as well as his calm guidance through the great shifts of my life.

"Do not grieve," Amun said to me. "Be pleased that he is here, for he is powerful!"

I looked at Odínn again.

"Bring down the Sun!" I said petulantly. He smiled broadly in his black beard and without turning or even a motion the Sun archetype was there in blinding aspect. The smile never left Odínn's face and I could feel his love.

"It has been my honor and privilege to work with you these past years," Amun said. "How fast you have progressed, though you probably are unaware of it. Remember that I will always be with you." He took a step back.

I thanked them both. Whatever I had planned was now gone from my mind.

I spent the rest of the day considering the situation. Part of me liked the idea of a new guide. Mostly I felt lonely. Once again, the change also portended new responsibilities. I quickly understood that Red Feather's guide needed to be balanced by someone similar in my world. And while Amun was probably just as powerful as Odínn, I suspected that Odínn had a more specialized knowledge to impart.

When I next journeyed to meet my guide, I was resigned to the change. Odínn intercepted me at a smooth rock face before I could even get to the landing and portal at which I always met Amun. The wall I had passed so often without a thought now held a pair of great wooden doors, iron-bound, flanked by torches, flung open to the inside. "The hall of the mountain king," I thought with a laugh. I looked up to where I would have joined Amun and saw him there, smiling his smile, holding a hand aloft. It filled me with sadness, but I turned to Odínn.

"This is our entrance," he said in a voice that was gentle yet commanding. It was the first time he had spoken. "Come!"

He led me up three broad stone steps and into an open forest of oak and pine very different from the Nile banks along which Amun and I always walked. We came to a circle of twelve oaks, greater than the rest, with a broad glade in the middle. It seemed to be mid-afternoon. The sun beamed between two of the trees.

"*You* bring the Sun down," Odínn said to me. I did so, and he nodded as if satisfied.

A few days later, I sought Amun again, telling Odínn my desire. He just smiled, and I climbed to the meeting place that already seemed to be slipping into memory. Amun stood there, and we walked again by the Nile to the spot where we had conversed so often or worked with the archetypes. He was gracious as always, but I felt our connection already disengaging. It had the flavor of meeting an old comrade once close but now long separated by the stream of time. He seemed fainter, as if there was barely enough energy to sustain the image. I gave him my deepest gratitude and love, which he returned. Months later I was still surprised to find myself missing him occasionally, though by then I had turned fully to Odínn. The portal to the old meeting place was itself now merely a rough granite surface.

)

Odínn was tall and broad. Whereas Amun dressed in rich purple robes and sometimes wore a great signet ring, Odínn favored unadorned black homespun. His long hair and beard were also black, but his eyes were gray. Was one missing or turned inward? Sometimes yes, sometimes no. Sometimes his hair was braided on both sides or singly in the back, but more often he wore it unbound. There was a sense of movement about him, as if miles were yet to be covered that day. Often it was hard to focus on his entire aspect at once.

I had not studied Norse mythology in any detail, though the outlines were familiar. Now I resisted doing so, not wanting to color my own experience and aware that the Norse Odin has steadfast followers even now. The first time I called him Odin he immediately corrected me. "Odínn!" leaving little doubt about the matter.

But I did grow curious. For one thing Odin figured strongly in a soul retrieval I did for a Swedish friend several months before. It surprised us both. Just a few days after I met Odínn, the friend sent me some lines from the Elder Edda in pure synchronicity.

Wounded I hung on a wind-swept gallows
For nine long nights,
Pierced by a spear, pledged to Odin,
Offered, myself to myself,
The wisest know not from whence spring
The roots of that ancient rood....

I had neither mentioned anything about my new experience nor discussed Odin since our work. Had I ever seen this? I didn't think so, yet the words were so familiar and resonated deeply. I read that the Odin of myth spent nine days suspended upside down from the Tree of Life or an oak in order to gain unique perspective, pierced by his own magic javelin. Another time he gave one of his eyes in a bargain for heightened perception. Two ravens named Thought and Memory were never far from him. I had to ask about it.

When I did, he seemed impatient. "Yes, yes, all that," he said, waving a large hand dismissively.

"Are you a god then?" I needed to know who or what I was dealing with now, though I had no doubt he was a guide. Red Feather had Smoking Mirror, apparently another god and a fearsome one at that. The whole situation confused me.

"Well it seems they made me into one and started a religion." We were walking through the oaks where it was always about three in the afternoon. He chuckled a bit ruefully and added, "But nothing like what they did to poor Jesus."

He said we had shared a life together, but the images he gave me were murky. It seemed ancient, there was snow, and I saw myself as a young assistant, accompanying him on vast rounds over hundreds of leagues, and then as an older man of some means offering food and shelter at my farmstead whenever he came by. There also seemed to be a strong connection with the Siberian way of shamanism, including visionary mushrooms. I did not see myself as a student, however, and Odínn's words to me were simply that as I had once helped him so he was now helping me.

By this point I was less interested in exploring past lives anyway. There were hundreds, most of them unconscious and unremarkable. I had worked extensively with those that seemed most relevant to this life and had also connected with certain lives in the "future." But my current life was the most important. Besides, too much effort spent engaged with other lifetimes can invite trouble. Our seeming amnesia exists for good reason.

Odínn's way was direct, both with me and when working with the archetypes. He had practical things to teach and could be impatient when I gave too much leeway to a demanding archetype. I consulted him about clients sometimes, as I had with Amun. In those cases, Odínn seemed interested in helping to expand my role beyond the basic energy work and its challenging aspects, again showing impatience when he felt I had mostly indulged clients' laziness and addiction to drama. He showed me how I could integrate astrology more directly into my healing practice using his sacred grove of twelve oaks, and softly guided me in my efforts to engage the Dark from a place that was neither attraction nor aversion. Once I asked him why Amun had not told me about Red Feather when I was suffering from his initial, unrealized presence.

"You're just now getting to this?" he rumbled. "It was because you never asked. You wouldn't have believed it anyway."

Something else concerned me: an assertion in *The Inner Guide Meditation* that one's fourth guide would always be female. Odínn didn't strike me as very feminine.

"That has caused some problems," he responded with a frown. "In your case it is better for you to work with my masculine aspect, but I can show you the female side if you prefer."

As I watched, his features softened, the beard disappeared, and he lost some stature. In his place stood a large, matronly woman who smiled at me warmly. She carried the same strength as the male Odínn, although somewhat softer around the edges.

"It is complicated," she continued as if nothing had changed. "At this stage the rules are less firm than for one's first guide. Either gender is possible." She launched into an astrological explanation, disregarding my surprise.

Finally I thanked her, saying that if it was all the same I was used to the male version. She laughed just as he did and slowly morphed back to the masculine.

Odínn's arrival also seemed generally coincident with the appearance of other teachers in my inner world, the Traveler and Arrow, people there to show me specific things beyond simple counsel. Though he never said anything about it, I found myself returning to a more direct approach to things in the inner world as well, dismantling the various structures, altars, and even cities I had created over years of experiment with archetypal energy and manifestation. It suddenly seemed like so much magic jewelry whose supposed powers were now only a burden.

Like the other guides, he never predicted or foretold other than to say that this particular time in planetary history is filled with possibilities; choices made now will be greatly magnified in the time to come. And he indicated that at least one of my subsequent guides, whenever that happens, is female.

26

Smoking Mirror

~February~
Waxing Moon in Gemini

"There is plenty of room for evil within good. And there's
plenty of room for good within evil. On the bright path,
darkness always follows you around. On the dark path, you
will be stalked by light. This is the nature of things."

— Mary Gardener[*]

So Red Feather had met my new guide. Now we needed to meet his
again. From that point they could proceed with their own work.
While I would have loved to follow them around to see what teachings
this great guide had to bestow, two things prevented me from doing so.

First, Red Feather always honored my guide work as a private af-
fair, never seeking to insert himself, though when it came to meeting
the Traveler or the Council he was eager. It remained a compartment
in my life where he rarely ventured and then only by invitation. I felt it
only proper to give similar respect to his personal work. A few boundaries were probably good for all.

Second, there was only so much time to devote to the inner world,
no matter how wonderful and vast. The queries I brought to my guide
regarding dreams, personal issues, clients, and other matters often
opened whole avenues that filled an entire session. Archetype work
could also be demanding. Further, in addition to the monthly Council
meetings, there was now the Traveler and his teachings. An average sitting took an hour or more each day. And while I appreciated traditions

---

[*] *Crossing into Medicine Country: A Journey in Native American Healing,*
by David Carson.

of much lengthier meditation, I neither lived in a monastery nor had the patience for longer sitting. My grandfather once spent time in a Zen monastery in Japan. His tales of rigor never inspired me to do the same.

But on this day Red Feather and I journeyed together. In the ice cave, he stopped and turned. "I have come here several times while you slept." He looked slightly sheepish. Perhaps he thought I might find his action disloyal.

I was quick to reassure him that if anything I was impressed by his boldness.

At the portal, he turned to me again. Pointing to the shifting symbols painted on the deerskin flap, he told me that they represented various gods in manifestation, the archetypes we were there to meet. He pushed through.

It was daytime and the landscape seemed little changed from our previous visit. Red Feather moved ahead more confidently and soon encountered his flicker. The bird emitted a single cry and flew off in its characteristic rise and fall as we followed. Soon we saw Black Hawk standing with Smoking Mirror. Red Feather and Smoking Mirror sat on the ground opposite each other while Black Hawk and I hung back a pace or two on each side. They bowed deeply and sat silently in each other's presence, eyes locked.

After what seemed like many minutes, Smoking Mirror raised his hand and brought down both Sun and Moon in the same human forms as before to join the circle. Finally Red Feather spoke.

"I ask you to bring down the Wheel."

It was difficult for me to determine whether he actually said "Wheel of Fortune" or used another name, but I knew he meant the archetypal force, one of whose manifestations or harmonics is the physical planet Jupiter. Smoking Mirror nodded approval and without any further motion a luminous figure suddenly appeared within the circle. I could feel Red Feather struggling to resolve the image, asking it to become more solid, allowing it to show itself in whatever way it would.

One's first encounter with an archetype requires some patience and strength. It is a moment when one also comes face to face with an aspect of oneself, though it is not merely a psychological projection. Quite possibly the archetype will be angry or even a monster—something we might prefer to project onto someone else. After that, meeting one's shadow figures is even harder and best left for a time when one has a better feel for the process.

I had long since worked through all of this for myself by the time Red Feather and I began our connection. He had seen me hold space for all kinds of energies to manifest in order to understand them better, yet I was concerned for him. I shouldn't have worried.

Soon, a regal-looking man in buckskin stood before him, eyes smiling. Red Feather proceeded flawlessly with the negotiations. In the end, the archetype handed Red Feather a small medicine pouch to be worn around the neck in order to help expand and manifest the path of the heart. Red Feather then had all the archetypes who were present speak in order to see where they stood in relation to each other and to begin bringing greater balance where necessary. At the end, they formed a circle of hands with Smoking Mirror. I could feel the energy rising in vibration until the guide abruptly broke the link. Red Feather thanked each archetype and they vanished, two quite dramatically.

Smoking Mirror turned to me, as if becoming aware of my presence for the first time.

"Yes, I am *that* Smoking Mirror. You might say I speak for Quetzalcoatl's other half, closer than a brother, more like the other side of the mirror. You know well enough that it is the victors who write history, which is why the name I bear is now dishonored and feared. Now, as Quetzalcoatl returns, so does Tezcatlipoca." His eyes narrowed and he looked at me closely. I felt uncomfortable, hot. Neither humor nor any sort of love came from him, but there was cool compassion. At least I did not feel unwelcome.

"Do you find me evil…or strong?" he asked.

I had no immediate answer.

"Think of your own new guide. Think of his story. Mine is similar." His eyes moved past my shoulder, and I realized that Odínn was there. This was interesting, but there was no time to ponder.

"Red Feather and I will step away," continued Smoking Mirror. "Wait one day for us." They disappeared.

I wasn't sure whether to stay there or to return the following day. But as I stood there I noticed the sun itself seemed to be arcing more quickly across the sky. I looked at Black Hawk, who was also with us. He returned a huge smile. I liked that guy.

Odínn eyed me impassively and then redirected my attention to the sky with his chin. Soon enough the sun sank into a low bank of clouds, firing them orange from within, turning their edges into liquid chrome, and then it was gone. A planet began to ascend low in the east. Stars emerged a few at time and then all at once, the sliver of new moon visible where the sun had recently set. Slowly the sky wheeled around the North Star, turning fast enough to make the occasional meteors come rapid fire.

I was familiar with time-lapse images of the changing sky on television and so forth, but watching the show in one's own real-life planetarium was more than breathtaking. Was this how rocks and trees experienced the passage of time?

When the sky began to brighten, I noticed a distant speck of fire. Had it been there all night? I didn't think so.

"I'm going there," I announced, and went quickly, followed by the others.

It turned out to be a large blaze, tended by Smoking Mirror himself, heating stones the size of his head and handing them to someone inside the nearby sweat lodge on the banks of an ice-crusted stream. He paid us no heed. As the sun rose above the hills, Red Feather suddenly burst forth and with a great whoop splashed into the water and laid down. He was glowing and steaming like one of the night's meteors. Smoking Mirror looked on approvingly and then turned on his heel and walked to me.

"Red Feather can come here on his own," he stated in a way that demanded a response.

I appreciated the confirmation and nodded.

"He is lucky to have you, for you consider his presence and connection a sacred trust." He waited for my reply, but I could only keep nodding. His presence was overwhelming.

"You needed a guide who could balance my power." He stopped again, his expression impenetrable, then added, "I say this in humility." Seeing that I understood, he then observed, "Your trip here was more for yourself than for him."

He was correct. I acknowledged his words, this time bowing in deep respect. He returned the bow and then went back to Red Feather, waving us off a short distance so they could converse privately. Was this how Red Feather felt when meeting my guides—out of place? Regardless, I was both reassured to see Red Feather in good hands on his own path and glad to get a few answers.

The god called Smoking Mirror presented some problems. I knew as little about Aztec and Mesoamerican cosmology as I did about the Norse gods, but I did know something about Smoking Mirror, or Tezcatlipoca. To put it mildly, his reputation was fearsome. He was a very dark god, sometimes called the twin of Quetzalcoatl, but whereas the latter was the god of light, music, and harmony in the Middle World, Smoking Mirror was associated with death, sorcery, and darkness. His name itself came from an ancient deception he had practiced against his brother. I also knew that even now there were men and women allied with the deity. Their arts were said to be "unhealthy."

Yet just as Odínn, my guide, was no god, neither was the being named Smoking Mirror whom I could see in the near distance. I suspected that the situation was similar. In some Norse lore, Loki, the dark trickster and slayer of Balder the golden god, was called Odin's brother or twin. The pattern fit, or mirrored. I also recalled my first thought on seeing Paqo at the outset of the Council meetings.

What I supposed and later found to be true was that Red Feather's guide had served during his time on Earth as mediator between humans and the Dark. Our western culture has made a practice of banishing the Dark, acknowledging only the Light, thereby binding our shadow side and everything associated with it to the concept of evil. When too much of what we would rather not see is shoved into the basement, it can re-emerge in unpleasant and confusing ways. Or it may become an unhealthy obsession. Better to address the Dark from a place that is neither fear nor attraction, which seemed to be Smoking Mirror's function.

)

Months later, during a workshop that addressed archetypal questions, I thought that inasmuch as a few of the other participants were presenting interpretations it might be interesting to embody Smoking Mirror, the god. After consulting Odínn, I journeyed with Red Feather for the first time since this day to his inner landscape and made a request of his guide.

"Are you sure?" he asked.

I nodded.

"This is no game. Remember I am not what you seek, but I will help modulate that energy so that you are not cooked, too much. The proper attitude is one of deep respect. The gift you bring is yourself. That is the only one he will accept," he added ominously. He gazed at me long enough that I wondered whether he was reconsidering.

"Prepare yourself," he said at last.

I followed his direction, eating little during the lunch break, opting to sit in deep meditation. I can only compare the experience to a drug. It came on subtly, filtering in from the edges of consciousness, like smoke. But as I sat through various presentations, I indeed felt the dark god enter and fully possess me in a way that was beyond anything I had experienced, including previous archetypal contacts. I felt my energy rise to an uncomfortable level, burning far too bright. My left leg began to hurt, a lot.

Unlike most of the others, I had not prepared anything and knew few specifics. When my turn came, something within began to tell the story of the great god Quetzalcoatl. Only this story was from his dark brother's perspective. How I, Smoking Mirror, caused Quetzalcoatl to look in the obsidian mirror at the distorted image I had prepared, an image he accepted at face value. How in horror the shining god fell from his pinnacle to become nothing but a begging drunkard. How the people who formerly praised him quickly rejected him. "What kind of god fouls himself and rolls in the dirt?" I asked. "I know you." Male and female alike they were only too happy to kick him down the road and set me in his place. While Quetzalcoatl roamed the world offering his gifts, I sat in the places of worldly power and used their own fear to enmesh them ever deeper in complicity.

It was an incredible perspective.

After fifteen minutes I had to stop or be crisped. A living blackness that I had never before experienced coiled through me. I understood its attractions in a way that had nothing to do with common polarities and definitions. There was a call for questions or comments. No one spoke. Perhaps people only saw an egotist and were hoping he was done. That was fine. Finally someone said, "It felt hot."

I sat down and thanked both the god and Red Feather's guide as the waves of energy began to diminish. A strong voice said, "Don't ask again."

I haven't.

)

All that was to come. Now Red Feather came up from his sweat, refreshed and cleansed. Smoking Mirror bowed slightly toward Odínn and me, then pivoted to intercept his protégé. After a few words Red Feather approached and we rose up into the sky, through bedrock and into the mouth of our own cave where the sun shone brightly. I felt as if I had just done a sweat of my own.

27

A Huaca!

-March-
New Moon Entering Aries

The new moon came on a beautiful evening. My wife and I thought it would be a good idea to do a fire. As the stars showed themselves, we opened sacred space and started the fire, feeling the lineages of the different directions join us as we invited them, watching the fire burn gold, and making our offerings and prayers at the proper moment. The weather was unseasonably warm but we were glad for it. The fruit trees were already beginning to flower, and we hoped that a late frost wouldn't nip the apricot blossoms again this year.

In the sweet morning, Red Feather and I went to join the Council. The day was just as beautiful in my valley.

He turned to me. "The Creator smiles on our endeavors."

His words were a surprise. We had never discussed such things specifically, but it felt right. Almost out of sight against the mare's tail clouds I could see the speck of an eagle.

We met Aquila and went to the Traveler's place. He was not present, though the ashes were warm, confirming what I thought I had seen several days earlier. I wondered how closely he monitored my activities. Our journey to the Crystal Cave was uneventful, traveling as we had done the previous time, except this occasion we simply materialized seated in place. Just one or two others were there with Arrow. The cave mouth was open and there was no fire.

Arrow seemed very pleased to welcome us. He noted my question about the entrance, twinkled, and said, "It is such a nice day." Then, regarding me for a moment, he asked with some emphasis, "How *are* you?"

"Okay, I guess."

"Really?"

"I'm fine."

"Really?"

I assessed myself and realized I felt very good.

"Blessed and happy."

"So I thought!" He turned to Red Feather. "And you?"

"I am well." Red Feather continued on to describe the meetings with his guide.

"Excellent!" said Arrow.

I asked about the watchers.

"This place is protected, but they key on your own doubts, which would be the only way in here for them. That is always the way of the best sorcerers and their servants. Make no mistake: there are some very good ones, but for the most part their motives keep them from operating effectively above a certain vibration, one that we have already passed."

By this time the full Council was seated. The door darkened and for a few moments there was nothing but black. Slowly our own fields softly illuminated the darkness and the cave itself began to luminesce. The love we felt for each other was tangible and sufficient. Finally Arrow turned to the Chinese fellow seated second on my left.

"Shining Wind! Will you make a fire?"

"With pleasure." He smiled broadly, then leaned forward and blew with force. A little past his lips the breath ignited in a stream of green fire that hit the center of the floor, blazing intensely.

"Impressive!" Arrow exclaimed. We watched as the dancing flames surged upward then settled and continued burning strongly. I think we were all impressed.

At last, Arrow directed us to join hands. We formed the thirteen-sided crystal.

"Bring in the white and black lights to activate your vision," he directed. "That is what pulls us forward."

We did so easily, formulating each light with our intent. I found myself standing by a great mountain torrent, reaching to cup its pure, sweet water. The vision lasted for a while until I returned to the cave to see the others awaking from similar visions. We dropped our hands and sat in reverie.

Arrow cleared his throat. "It seems the Secret is out," he said with a grin.

He was referring to a movie and book that were popular at the moment—at least in the English-speaking world. The Secret, supposedly revealed for the first time, presented the laws of attraction with evangelical fervor, showing how to manifest the things and relationships one desires in life. The title and presentation were quite clever, nor was the premise incorrect.

"It is nothing new, but its success points to the readiness of humanity to accept these ideas," said Arrow. "How else to reach them except by beginning in the material world? It is part of the Unfolding. But you have always known about this and are less interested in objects than in the soul's journey and helping the Earth in her own manifesting." He laughed. "Anyone here want a new car?"

He grew serious again. "We will use our crystalline shape to pierce the first five upper worlds. We will bring down the energy of Heaven."

I knew this practice and had done it three times in my life. It is a powerful but tricky thing, not to be undertaken lightly. The energy he referred to cannot be easily controlled or directed. Its effect is to harmonize, rebalance, and heal, but its course can be unpredictable. Each time I had brought it down for personal transformation I felt the effects spread dramatically through my life, though a teacher talked about also using it for his tomato plants. One time, carelessly, I placed a weather stone in the energy field in order to bring some relief to a parched summer. Within three hours a thunderstorm emerged from the empty sky. The downpour rendered a nearby highway impassable.

In my training they are called *huacas*, a Quechua word loosely translated as "power spot." Whereas my first huaca was just to see whether I could do it and what effect it might have, I undertook the subsequent two with serious and well-considered intent. I sometimes thought of it as the "nuclear option." To my knowledge it can only be used for positive effect, however.

Arrow's aim seemed audacious. Moreover I had never done a huaca as a group. I was eager to see how this might work. We joined hands and formed our crystal. When it felt strong, we began moving our focus and intention upward from the top of our mountain. Pushing the boundaries of each upper world with ease, we passed in succession through the levels of stone, plant, animal, and then the ancestors, finally bursting into the fifth world, the domain of the ascended masters and avatars in their luminous cities. At that point I felt a tremendous rush of energy. A pillar of electric blue light shot straight down the path we had created from our Crystal Cave, accompanied by a noise like a million bees. For the first time I was aware that the energy actually came from somewhere above the fifth world—perhaps a sixth heaven or beyond, comprehensible only in energetic terms. My attention dropped back to our cave and I tried to look across the room. The blue pillar obscured everything. I was awestruck and could barely hear Arrow shout, "Hold the circle!"

The energy stuttered several times as our own focus wavered. Then it stabilized and held steady. As with my personal versions there came a point when the huaca was unwavering enough to withdraw my intent. We dropped hands, marveling at this immense, living power. In comparison, even the energy of the galactic center seemed just a reflection. The hum had dropped to a point where we could hear each other again, though it was still difficult for me to see the opposite side of the cave.

"You must feed this for the next twenty-eight days, each in your own way, once a day," said Arrow over the sound. I noted how the huaca had activated the entire mountain and again how the entire web of planetary meridians was being informed.

"What is unbalanced will be rebalanced," he continued. "What needs healing will be healed. What must come into the light will be brought forth."

Suddenly I was aware of other groups performing similar actions in different parts of the globe. I felt the members of our circle notice too.

"It only takes a few," I heard Arrow say. "Each is doing it in its own way. Ours is not the only way, only what is most true for you. Those who insist there is but one path merely display their own ignorance. Those who go beyond words in their insistence display their desperation and absence of faith in their own truth."

We basked in the huaca energy briefly until its strength started to feel slightly uncomfortable. People were stirring.

"Leave when you wish," said Arrow.

Soon only two others remained: Paqo, with whom I exchanged a few thoughts through the blue pillar, and Shining Wind. Even Arrow was gone. The door stood open, but I wanted a word with Shining Wind and was glad he had stayed. I moved next to him so we could speak better.

"What do you know about dragons?"

He turned toward me. "We in the East have not suppressed that energy as you have. Now it is slowly returning for you."

Indeed, I had noted as much in my own inner work, as well as with clients. The energy seemed to come from a holding place of deep concealment.

"We have worked with it—we never stopped. It is an ancient and powerful force, and it is conscious. Different qualities are most evident as color variation."

"Are they connected to the Rays?" I asked.

"I am not sure what you mean. But there are at least twelve. As many as seven can go in the body," he said, scanning me. "The other five are too strong, though perhaps they too are connected to higher chakras. They have fire, but it comes from a higher source, not directly from them. This is a common misunderstanding. And," he added as a follow-up to a comment Arrow had made some time ago, "the strongest is the Black Dragon!" His eyes were shining.

I had more questions, but he turned to take in Red Feather and began his own questions. I told him our story in brief.

"How interesting for you both."

"We do not fully understand it ourselves."

"That is the best part. I am honored to meet you," he said, extending a hand toward Red Feather. They clasped hands, and then it was past time to leave. The huaca was simply too intense.

We returned the way we had come. The Traveler was waiting for us and had kindled a small fire, despite the coming warmth of the day. He stood as we emerged from the nearby trees.

"Welcome back."

28

The Green Wave

-April-
New Moon in Aries

A long month passed. At sunset, Red Feather and I made our way down the long passage to the door to Elsewhere. He had not come here for several weeks and immediately noticed the difference.

Since I first found it, the door had always been nondescript, a brown metal utility entrance of the type found at the back of any office building. It amused me that such a magic portal could be so plain. But two weeks prior I found it suddenly transformed to a broad, wooden door, reinforced with black metal studs and bands. A great bar crossed its width as a latch. The doorway itself was now arched and two wall torches set in iron brackets illuminated the area.

"Interesting," Red Feather remarked, looking at me. Certainly that was the least of a number of sudden changes to my inner landscape, several of which left me gasping. Some features had just disappeared. I felt as if things were bumped up a level but was unsure what that meant. Such is the effect of a huaca.

Within, it was also dusk, as if we were now in linear time rather than outside it or slightly ahead of it. I asked the protector whether he could accompany us, but he replied that if we journeyed entirely through rock there was little for him to do. He gave me a picture indicating that it would be difficult for him to remain in stone while the Council was in session.

Looking into the darkening valley, I could see the winking fire. Overhead, there were stars. We dropped down to meet Aquila and moved up the valley floor, following the stream, which was bursting and roaring with snow melt. At the fire, the Traveler noted the concern in our eyes and laughed out loud.

"I needed to get out," he said innocently. "Fine night." I wasn't convinced that he was there just to take the air, but he added, "I'll keep this fire going for you."

I felt the pull of the Council, and we journeyed to the cave in the same way as on the last several occasions, emerging from the wall immediately behind our place. A fire burned and the cave mouth was open, though no one entered that way. Arrow was in his place, lost in the fire. Outside I could see the last rim of red over the mountains across the valley and a star or two. Some Council members were already there, yet I found it hard to focus on them or the ones who arrived after us.

My own recent shifts had been so significant that I worried whether I would be able to do anything on this night. Now, depression welled from a deep place I was unable to access. The huaca was merely an echo, though it had only just disappeared. During the past month, I started each day by "feeding" it through my medicine bundle and could sense the energetic connection running as soon as I opened it. No doubt that link affected my own life, perhaps catalyzing all the inner-world changes I was experiencing. On the twenty-seventh day I felt it start to collapse, which was normal. The next day it was gone.

Raising my head, I realized that all members were present and brought myself to make eye contact. Some just nodded and smiled, others exchanged mental greetings. Alice said, "My best to your wife." The African man smiled but also seemed preoccupied. I wondered whether he shared my mood. No doubt the huaca energy had affected us all.

"Join hands," Arrow commanded.

The energy rose effortlessly. I became aware that the huaca was active again — the column of living energy rushing straight down from the fifth world, filling our cave with bluish light. We sat in its strength before releasing hands reluctantly and carefully. The huaca continued.

"This is how it will be now, whenever you, the Council, are joined. *You* create the column of energy. You *are* the column of energy. It stays," Arrow said above the sound. "You have done well to sustain it over the past month, each in your own way."

The energy was intense but somewhat more bearable than before. Its flow was constant, like being in some kind of energetic downpour only nothing like any of the earlier energies we had run. I felt it lighting the planetary meridians. Arrow directed us to join hands again. "We will work with more colors, using this crystal mountain to broadcast a color, an energy. It will be the energy in this cave, transmuted by you. It pulses through the Earth's meridians now, but we seek to radiate a specific vibration outside of that. What is softest and easiest?"

"Green," a number of us responded.

"Of course. Picture green waves emanating like ripples from a stone cast into a pond."

We tried, envisioning green waves moving out from our mountain. Arrow soon stopped us. We could all feel that it was only partially effective, diminishing with distance.

"Perhaps I gave the wrong image," he said. "Try one green pulse."

We did so, drawing effortlessly on the huaca energy and felt a single green swell of healing roll around the Earth to return undiminished. I also experienced it in my physical body sitting in meditation, a sensation of love and well-being centering in the heart.

"We will learn to focus this energy," Arrow continued. "It is very powerful! Send another pulse. One pulse."

This time it seemed more specific and more effective.

"Another!"

In the space of a second, the wave moved out in every direction from the crystal mountain and returned, washing through our cave with a sound that matched the huaca, only at a different yet harmonious pitch. We all felt the planetary consciousness, that totality of all beings and Earth herself, shift slightly.

"Nicely done!"

"What about the other lights, especially the black one?" someone asked.

"They are active," Arrow responded. "Call in the black light."

We followed his direction, using our intent and tasting the difference. It felt unformed, much broader in spectrum, emanating from a different point than the huaca.

"It is useful," Arrow said. "We will learn to focus that too." He paused for us to continue sampling. The huaca energy and the black light didn't seem to conflict but neither was there immediate harmony.

"This is the first time in a very long time that particular energy has been broadcast as you have done—a very long time," he said, referring to the green, and let his statement sink in. "A few ancient civilizations used these lights for healing, but its potential for misuse is obvious. You are all people of integrity, yet it would be an error to assume you know best. For now, continue as we have done: hold in mind simply that your efforts are for the highest good..." he stopped, peering around the circle for emphasis, before adding loudly, "and without attachment to specific outcome," and paused again. "Later, we will work with more focused beams. Now, let's try purple."

Envisioning a purple surge emanating from our mountain, we sent a pulse outward and felt it return almost instantly after blanketing the Earth. It was completely dissimilar, sharper, a different harmonic from the green.

"That is a taste, and enough," Arrow said as we all sat back and exchanged smiles.

His words came as a relief. We had been at our work quite a while, and I was tired. Arrow stood as if to stretch but simply checked the cave mouth. The entrance began a slow dissolve from dark wall to dark sky. He looked older than I had thought earlier. Still standing, he cast his gaze around the room.

"You are all undergoing bodily transformations. It can feel strange, sometimes confusing, not always comfortable. Let it happen. You are becoming crystals, luminous beings in a sense. Each of you is here for specific reasons, with certain talents, but you are also facets in the crystal the twelve of you form in the crystal mountain. Crystals within crystals!" He looked around again. I saw some faint smiles, which gave me comfort. I wasn't the only one.

We were done. Several members disappeared immediately, none using the entrance. Red Feather and I lingered for a bit. As soon as the first members departed, the huaca reduced its intensity, though more in its potential than its presence. Soon, I too felt the need to leave. The huaca energy was just too strong. We went toward the front, which was now fully open. It looked so inviting, and I was tired of moving through distances of rock.

"I wouldn't recommend that," Arrow said. "What we do is now well known." He said nothing else, leaving us to consider what sort of unwelcome excitement waited out there.

We returned the way we came.

The Traveler was at his fire. "Sit! Relax! Let me look at you, both of you."

We sat and he cast an eye over us each in turn. Satisfied about something, he turned his face toward the night sky.

"Beautiful night."

29

Highest Destiny

~May~
New Moon in Taurus

Although the new moon occurred a day earlier, the following morning seemed the correct time to join the Council. As I set my intent, connected with Red Feather, and focused my consciousness, I happened to glance out the window. The weather was warming up. Today there was even a chance of afternoon thunderstorms. I could see some broken clouds and was about to begin the journey when something caught my attention.

Two eyes regarded me from the edge of one of the clouds, becoming more distinct as I returned the gaze. A face began to resolve. It was not a friendly face. I looked away for a few moments, not wishing to strengthen the connection. When I looked again I only saw two slightly darker spots where there had been eyes, quickly being absorbed into the moving cloud mass. I felt Red Feather's attention directed there as well, though neither of us mentioned it.

Past the portal we found ourselves standing above the valley just before dawn. It was quite chilly there, unlike my outer world, and I could see Red Feather's breath. The sight startled me, though we often experienced deep cold in the inner world. I felt his amusement.

"Well, I *am* alive."

The Traveler was absent. We journeyed through rock directly to the Crystal Cave. A steady green fire illuminated the space well, which was helpful because there was only a rough rock wall in place of the entrance. Only Arrow and the African man were present.

Our arrival did not interrupt their conversation, but Arrow soon looked toward me then back to the African and said, "You two have experienced the most changes recently. Things come up you can't even name. As your vibration increases you shed skin — almost literally." He nodded toward me again, acknowledging a recent experience. "Some isn't even yours in a personal sense."

The African and I exchanged a look. I finally got that his name was Amáne and that he was from West Africa.

"Which country?" I asked.

"I am more aligned with my people and place than with the newest dictator or politician," he said, smiling a little sadly. I understood that the place he referred to was part of more than one country. He inclined his head to speak again, but Arrow drew our attention.

"Step into the fire. You first," he said, fixing on me.

I did so, careful not to drag Red Feather along. It was a cool, cleansing flame. I soon felt slightly more elevated. After I finished, I watched Amáne do the same. When he resumed his place, I turned to Arrow.

"Who is Victoria, the woman who sits on your right?"

"She is from here but not here, like the Traveler. There are no words yet to describe this."

I looked down, considering what this could possibly mean and was deep in contemplation when I realized that the other Council members had arrived and were seated. Arrow was looking around the circle slowly.

"We began not very long ago. You are all here by choice and ability. It has been a learning process as you realized your capabilities. Together we are an important link, just as other links are equally essential. You influenced possibilities and outcomes. Easily. Some things you saw and altered simply by allowing different paths. We talked about dreaming worlds into being and energized those forms. All of that is preliminary. Now the real work begins.

"Earth is at a tipping point. That is being said a lot these days. We each carry visions of possible negative and positive threads and outcomes — beautiful or terrible — and are grasping at the best ones we can perceive. All are potential. But consider: all those dreamings are limited by our own minds and inevitable ideas — conscious and unconscious — of good and bad. I can see your wonderful visions. Our work here unites them in common purpose, yet I must remind you: holding a vision is not the same as imposing it. Do you understand the difference?

"Your intent in this matter and as Council members must be impeccable!

"Now what we must also do is hold a space for her highest destiny, which she herself will choose. Then it will be our task to harmonize with it. She awakens from a long sleep, 26,000 years to be exact. Whatever name you choose—there are many—it is a long time to slumber. The awakening is not immediate. Think how long it takes some of you to wake from just one night. All the precious glories and tragedies and kings and queens and prophets of human history during this great sleep are just prelude to what now comes—the emergence of a new human and a new Earth."

He stopped and gazed into the fire as if watching the entire span recapitulate in a few instants, then raised his chin sharply.

"Link!"

As we joined hands, green flame engulfed the chamber. I saw what I can only describe as Gaia, the Earth Spirit, appear in the center. She was not a round planet or a bulbous fertility goddess, or even a fixed person or figure. The vision was a shimmering flame, sometimes a human form, sometimes just a face, expanding and contracting with a slow pulse or breath. We sensed her own surprise followed by something akin to a yawn and then growing awareness and rising consciousness. We held space for an awakening green light of shifting hues, itself enfolding the vining strands of other awarenesses, animals, spirits, humans, plants, and rocks. It became a great pathway among many pathways that formed the evolution of Spirit-consciousness Itself. Finally the green subsided slightly, and we all dropped our gaze to the floor to honor what we had experienced. Long moments passed.

"Link!" Arrow said, abruptly as before.

Now the light bathing the cavern slowly shifted from green to indigo. I was aware of its near-physical presence in the form of cool emotion and deep information very different from the green light.

"Send out one ping," said Arrow as if he were a submarine captain.

We emitted an indigo wave that rolled around the planet in the space of a few seconds.

"Another!"

The second wave seemed easier and longer.

"Another!"

The third lingered even more than the second.

"Sustain!"

This time we held it much as a singer might have held a note. I saw that we had all risen slightly above the cavern floor and felt the indigo light strongly in my physical body.

"There *will* be miracles!" I heard Arrow proclaim from a great distance.

We were unwilling to release, holding the light for what seemed like several minutes. Arrow finally broke the chain, and I found myself seated on the chamber floor again. The indigo light continued as an echo.

"It is a ray," Arrow said grandly, "a dragon, a consciousness. It is a tuning for Mother Earth to help her with her awakening. We will go through all the colors, even the unknown ones. This is our real work." He stopped for a few minutes to allow our meditation, smiling the whole time.

"You will continue to feel and transmit this color," he said more quietly, "simply because of our linking here today. We meet again in two weeks, at the full moon — a blue moon!" He smiled at the thought and then frowned, adding very seriously as if addressing an office work group, "You might want to adjust your schedules accordingly." His tone raised a few heads, which made him laugh again. "After that we may meet at the new moon as well. Don't touch that dial!" Some people smiled. He twinkled but then turned serious again.

"With this tuning, things will shake loose. Be aware of it. Avoid dismay and fear nothing, but remember this: you are not invulnerable. Maintain awareness at every level." He cast his eyes to the floor and was silent.

I did the same. There was much to absorb. When I finally looked up everyone was gone except for Amáne and Victoria.

"You are three of the four who join us in waking life rather than in their dreaming," Arrow observed. "For each of you there are different reasons." He turned to me then to the others.

"Do not fear," he reiterated. "Walk in beauty!"

I remained a little longer to discuss the matter of publishing what seemed would soon be a finished book. Then Red Feather and I returned to the valley.

"I am grateful to have experienced this day," he said looking at me directly. "We indeed walk in beauty."

I opened my eyes and raised them to the window. Outside, the sky was cloudless turquoise.

30

Lunacy

~June~
Full Moon in Sagittarius

A blue moon is simply an extra full moon within a solar year, yet it always seems worthy of attention. On this night, my wife and I welcomed the moonrise with a fire, honoring as well the presence of Jupiter, Mars, and Venus. It was a beautiful early summer night in the mountains. Our ceremonies tended to be somewhat impromptu, usually just the two of us, but they were never lonely. Tonight there was a full complement of visitors and friendly spirits within our sacred space.

The days leading up to full moon were difficult for us both. I moved through elation to depression almost manically. Several times Odínn counseled me to allow events to unfold rather than try to manipulate or constrain them. Yet I was also heedful of Arrow's caution from the last meeting. Most recently I felt particularly distant from any source of optimism. I wondered again if there was another will involved, perhaps some kind of attack. I checked my house defenses and consulted the protector. No, nothing was aimed at my family or me directly, but the protector did show me an interesting picture: shadow forms rapidly crisscrossing the sky in near panic. Something had come unhinged.

I got a clear understanding when it would be best to meet the Council. At dawn Red Feather and I journeyed to the valley and a beautiful morning. The protector reminded me that if we proceeded to the Council through the Earth it would be difficult for him to wait within solid rock. Waiting outside might attract attention. He also drew my attention to the sky in the outer world and again I saw the contrails of confused and angry shadow servants seeking to hold the old fabric together. I still had no answers about them or their masters, partly because I felt that too much curiosity would attract an equal amount of attention.

The Traveler was there, as I had hoped. The full moon had become our regular meeting time for his mentoring. Now I wasn't sure when we would meet. He sat on the ground as though before a fire, except there was none.

"Why make a fire? It's summer," he said seeming to explain the obvious. I appreciated his effort but couldn't share the humor. He looked at me carefully and steadily, then said, "What is dying in you is your desire for recognition."

I knew exactly what he meant.

He continued to assess me. "I will return soon," he said finally and faded away.

I thought he might reappear. When he didn't, I nodded to Red Feather. We dropped into the Earth with our intent set on the crystal mountain. Moving through the rock felt like a cleansing of sorts. I could feel bits of heavy emotion sticking to the little quartz particles as we filtered through the granite matrix. It reminded me of cleansings I had done for people by taking them to the stone world, the first of the five upper worlds. Did this journey also take place outside of time?

There was no time to consider the question, for we emerged at our place in the Council circle. We were the first. Arrow's head was bowed on his chest, as if sleeping, though he nodded slightly at our arrival. Green fire lit the chamber as usual. I had questions, yet it felt better to sit in stillness. It took a while for the others to arrive. When they did, it was in several groups in close succession. A final member came alone. We exchanged wordless greetings. The atmosphere of expectation was something I hadn't felt since our first meetings.

Arrow leaned forward and reached into the green fire, withdrawing a glowing handful. Passing it to me, he said, "Take some and pass it around."

I noted that as it passed from hand to hand the fire was undiminished, though each of us had an amount nearly equal to the original. It felt cool yet alive. I put some in my heart chakra, and then noted Arrow motioning me to put more in my root chakra. I spread the rest around my auric field like a wash, giving some to Red Feather as well. When all had finished, Arrow spoke.

"Welcome, welcome! This is new. You are adept at working with the new moon, the time of setting intent. Now we will have a different taste. We will work with this moon energy in its fullness." He drew himself up, clearly relishing the subject. "The moon is like a beloved but mysterious grandmother. She is usually nearby but often we're not sure where. Then she turns up at the most unexpected moments. Sometimes she welcomes you with open arms."

Someone sent around a picture of being engulfed in a smothering hug, which made us all laugh.

"Make it your business to know where she is," Arrow continued, "even during the day. It will help you stay conscious of your own emotional processes and aware of her influence. Now join hands."

As we linked, I could feel the indigo light but there was something else. The cave suddenly filled with the bright silver of moon glow. Arrow was right; it was different. Bathing in its beauty, we heard him say, "We will not transmit this light. That would be too much. Just get a taste. It is living silver."

Soon we released hands, but the light hardly diminished at all. It was intoxicating.

Arrow smiled. "It is a blessing that she is not full all the time. You are having a hard time concentrating even now!"

I was glad to hear him say so. He allowed us time to refocus.

"She helps to energize and release those things that need enlightenment—and by this I mean brought into the light—in their proper time and amount. Think what might happen if her course were different…." He trailed off without finishing the thought. Now he was very serious. I wondered if he was alluding to an earth change, such as a polar shift. He seemed lost in something unsaid or to be struggling with his own thought tangents. With an effort, he returned to the Council.

"Project your minds to her."

We sent our thoughts to the moon.

"She is not dead. People love to say that because it makes things seem simpler. In fact it cuts them off from mystery. She is alive! But her purpose is different from that of the sun."

With my mind probing the lunar interior, I experienced the truth of his words.

"Where does her light originate? On one level it is from the Central

Sun of our galaxy—she has a direct connection. But of course she also filters or refracts certain aspects of our own sun's unfailing light—just like all the planets." He stopped again for us to consider his words. Then he leaned into the circle a little, hands on his knees, to emphasize the next point.

"The full moon is when dreams, not intent, are most easily manifested. It is not a celebration of anything; it is a festival—the festival of dreams! Do you understand the difference? Now then, let us remember our vision and dream it again. Join hands. We are bringing these visions to Mother Earth as an offering for her highest destiny."

The silver light intensified to the point that it outshone the green fire in the center of the chamber. On a physical level I felt good to the point of giddiness.

"Yes it is hard to focus," I heard Arrow say from a great distance. "Don't force it."

We must have remained there for some time. I returned to my simple vision of pure waters running in a living wilderness and heard the ever-present beer-commercial refrain from my youth, complete with beating tom-tom, "from the land of sky-blue waters." I had loved that image and always thought it might be possible to find such a place. There was even a bear in the ad, if only a caricature. Now I was walking in the land of sky-blue waters. From pure water everything else would flow. I thought about humankind's unrelenting assault on the wild places and the wild things in our planet and in ourselves. It was a war of exiles on the Garden, our real home, executed ferociously and fueled by endless fear and hatred.

I do not know how long I dwelled in that vision. At a certain point, Arrow returned us from our dreaming.

"Our Grandmother Moon…. She is not the queen to our sun's king. More like a wise but mysterious feminine counselor—or perhaps an oracle. What some take as wildness or the untamed is just the tip of her knowledge and counsel, beyond words, thoughts and images slippery as fish but pregnant with wisdom. It is a different language, an intoxicated wisdom.

"It is essential to bring this wild wisdom into awareness and allowance now. It is not always pretty—especially now because it has been suppressed with violence for so long. Many will call it chaos because it transgresses the boundaries of how they think things are supposed to be. And here is an important thing to keep in mind as well. The untamed should not be taken as an end in itself simply because it seems to oppose the established ways. Nor is it a matter of feminine versus masculine. It needs to be brought in for balance." He looked at us carefully. "We bring it in to enable a releasing, the unburdening of our Earth."

Falling silent, he allowed his chin droop to his chest like an old man overcome with fatigue. We considered his words. Then he raised his head, alert as ever, and said sharply, "Keep this in mind as the changes multiply. Do not fear!" He gave us a stern look then grinned. "Of course, it's hard to fear when it feels like a party. Join hands again and hold your vision once more. We will dream the Earth into being."

Again I was in an untamed land of pure water and grasped the vision tightly. When I had wandered in that dream long enough to notice minute details, I opened my eyes and saw silver filling our cave more intensely than ever.

We released our hands and reveled in silver. It was indeed a party.

Finally Arrow said, "Next meeting, two days after the new moon."

And then we were done. Slowly, reluctantly, people began leaving. I lingered with the intention of asking the questions I put off earlier, but being in the silver light somehow diminished their pull. What was so urgent, anyway?

When only a few of us remained, Arrow turned on me with a knowing smile. "It goes well, does it not?" I laughed.

"Yes."

31

Through the Front Door

Perhaps it was because the Council met twice in one month or because of other events in my life, but I sensed rising momentum. I wondered whether it extended beyond me and if I could flow gracefully with the strengthening current. Was there any choice?

On this morning, feeling anything but graceful, I asked Red Feather to steady me down the passageway to the valley. I was still depleted from client work and would have preferred a different time, yet Arrow had been quite specific about our next meeting. There was no alternative. I had checked. I felt a hand at my back—an unusual sensation in the physical. It helped. Lifting the great iron deadbolt and swinging the door inward, we saw a glorious morning.

At the valley rim, I queried the protector about recent events that touched a recurrent issue. Why couldn't he guard me more when it came to certain types of energies I sometimes took on during client sessions? A common response would be that I had some kind of affinity. If so it ran deep—much deeper than anyone had been able to reach. I had learned much from these unsought experiences, of course, and sometimes wondered if they were part of my path. Regardless, it was never pleasant.

"I can protect you from external attack, especially when you are unaware of it," he told me, "but much less so when it comes to working with the spirits and entities you extract from people or places. In those cases your contact is too direct and immediate for my intervention."

That made sense, though it didn't offer any solutions.

I looked down into the valley and noted a wisp of smoke. The Traveler's presence added to my premonitions. I asked the protector to accompany us and arrived at the fire with Aquila and Red Feather. He smiled to see us all.

"Quite a committee!" Then without hesitation, he said, "As you guessed, we will go through the front door. I am here to help. Use your invisibility."

I had learned recently that at least one other Council member was also his protégé, but there was no time to ask now. In a moment we were crouched on the mountaintop across the stony valley from the cave. Far off I could see shadow forms patrolling the face of the crystal mountain and the open space between us. But where the cavern mouth should have been there was only a smooth wall of stone with nothing to indicate an opening. I also saw for the first time that the Traveler had his own protector. Recalling his earlier words, I returned to the present business.

For many months none of the Council members had entered or departed by the front door, as the Traveler called it. Yet hadn't Arrow also told us we were beyond this sort of thing and that our purposes were now obscure to those who first tried to stop us? I was confused, further recalling some of his other warnings.

"No thought. I will stay here with your protector," said the Traveler. And then there was silence. The watchers already seemed alert to our presence. Two of them were drifting in our direction.

I allowed all thoughts to drain away and after checking with Red Feather slowly moved over the valley as a fine mist. I had not practiced this form of invisibility since using it here, but right away I remembered that an absence of thought allowed me to disperse even these particles. Conversely, the occurrence of a random image or idea seemed to bring them closer. Red Feather was also experimenting, carefully. Without emotion, I noted that the watchers who had been drawn to our mountaintop now were moving off. I found this aspect of invisibility intriguing as well as strangely peaceful and almost forgot the watchers. After a time, we were at the rock face that obscured the cave mouth. So this is what it looked like from the outside. Filtering through the barrier, I noted that it was indeed rock but rock formed with intent.

"How artful. I need to learn this," I thought, before realizing my error. We emerged from its matrix and flowed over to our spot, coalescing into regular form.

Arrow turned toward us. "Good."

About half of the members were present, with the soundless green fire floating an inch off the floor. At intervals a few others slowly manifested through the door, while the rest arrived through the walls or the floor directly in their places. Arrow greeted each in turn, then allowed silence to fall.

Suddenly he raised his head as if to a signal. "Welcome!" His eyes were shining. "You have all been engaged in demanding work. I am grateful for your presence. Let us harmonize."

We formed a circle of hands. It felt good, and I was aware of a silver light rising, perhaps a vestige of our previous work. Arrow broke the circle finally.

"Many of you have found recently that you no longer walk in fear. You have found you can recognize and anticipate problems and that even in the worst situations you have the tools and capacity to deal with them." He appraised us and then cracked a large grin. "What a relief! There is a place for fear as a means to deal with a dangerous situation in a particular moment. Very useful, in fact," and he sent around a picture of himself running energetically from a charging bear. We laughed. "Yet most of what we call fear is just anticipation. Instead of focusing on an unpleasant outcome, choose a better one, or think of the unpleasant one in different terms. Our fear only blinds us and allows us to be manipulated." He allowed us to absorb his words.

"Join hands," he said finally. "We will go to the indigo light, and then the violet!"

The indigo light! I had almost forgotten about it. Reaching indigo was easy, but violet was difficult. It seemed to sputter in the chamber like a reluctant pilot light. At last Arrow dropped my hand simultaneously with Victoria's as if in disgust. He smiled though.

"Why violet and not red?" he asked.

It was something I had wondered. I was feeling the same question from several of the others. The human body's primary energy centers ascend from the base of the spine to the top of the head. Each is identified with a color of the rainbow from red at the base to white or violet at the crown. In certain healing work it is common to begin with the lowest affected chakra.

"Our planet has chakras too," Arrow went on. "But right now she needs this color, this vibration. Unlike bodywork, this healing needs to proceed from the top. She needs to be reinformed of her connection to Spirit, to the stars and her celestial family. Besides," he added as an aside, "there is too much red anyway. She needs balance. We will come to red soon enough."

We made another attempt, this time with more success, starting with a single pulse and then another before moving to a longer note. The violet was unsteady and kept verging on white. Yet for a tiny moment I felt that a million human spirits were reminded of their divinity.

"Violet is difficult," Arrow said when the circle disengaged, "but you can do it." He made quick eye contact with each of us to emphasize his encouragement. "For now, we will just sit in community."

His suggestion lightened the mood and suddenly there were smiles. It seemed as if there should be some food.

"Who has something to share?"

The African woman spoke at once. "I have wished to bring the Council some news," she said with a smile. "The village elder whose heart we strengthened now has three young students."

It was good to hear of some of the small effects of our work, and the mood brightened even more. She shared some mental pictures.

Then the Amazonian spoke. "Our trees thrive."

Again there were smiles, and he too shared a few images.

On my left Emeen raised her head. I noticed she did not share our mood. There always seemed to be a sort of purple tinge about her, which I enjoyed somehow. Now it was deeper.

"War again," she said sadly, quietly, and put out some pictures of desperate situations with which she seemed very familiar.

The mood darkened again as we considered. Arrow spoke.

"Yes, things are coming loose. The dark old thought forms are seeking to retain their hold. Fear feeds them, and it is their fear we feel in turn. It is strong."

"I am not in fear as much as concern for the suffering and destruction I see coming," the woman replied.

"Remember that we are all star beings," Arrow replied, "connected and counseled by our brothers and sisters who are still there. Call them archangels, if you wish." He grasped Victoria's hand, then mine, and looked to us to complete the circle. Perhaps it was part of his answer.

This time we were able to bring up a strong violet light and to transmit it from the crystal mountain. We saw our living planet bathed in it and could sense her remembering her larger connections, or advancing to a greater understanding just as we were remembering ours. It was very real, intensifying as we sustained the color and the vibration. Strange information came in, nonverbal, nonphysical, an even stronger remembering of divinity. The phrase "spirit beings having a human experience" now came more strongly to mind. I saw the planetary meridians illuminated with violet light and understood why Arrow could say that there was an imbalance. Our planet and its inhabitants all seemed hungry for this light.

We reached a point where we could no longer sustain our efforts and the circle broke. The violet light lingered, slowly fading in pulses until only the green light of the fire colored our chamber.

"Leave as you like," Arrow said. "If you choose the front, do it slowly and in invisibility. Most of all, do it without fear. Do it with artistry, competence, and certainty of your connection to Spirit!"

After a few moments, people began departing quietly. I asked Arrow how to proceed with what might soon be a completed book.

"Your instincts are good," he said in response to the options I presented. "We will let you know more later. Keep writing."

There was that "we" again. Did his vague response merely reflect the possibility that "we" hadn't decided anything quite yet?

He offered a warm smile and turned to face me more directly. "You did a great healing," he said, referring to events three days earlier. "I know it was hard for you to be here today and that you are still feeling the effects. The world is better for it."

"Thanks," I replied, "though it would have been nice to be paid for it." I was pleased to get confirmation of what I had been trying to understand, having dealt with something truly nasty and dangerous and taking an energetic hit in the process. Now admitted to myself that I was still slightly irked about how the business aspect had unfolded. My unthinking response embarrassed me.

"Yes." Arrow said. "Well, hold the thought that you will be paid. And note how you have been sustained lately."

He was right. I appreciated that he smiled again.

Red Feather and I rose to leave, approaching the front. The rock was just as solid as before. I wondered who was responsible, as Alice had already left. Molecule by molecule, we passed into the sunlight. Several watchers were there, facing outward. One passed close to our dispersed forms, but we stayed motionless, thoughtless, in stillness. After what seemed like many minutes, we drifted with infinite leisure over the valley.

At one point, there was a rushing noise from above and to the right. A watcher whistled directly through me. Sitting in meditation, I felt it in my gut as a residue of heavy, dense energy, manifesting as a dull ache. Without opening my eyes or anything more than slight acknowledgment, I slowly released the packet of darkness into the Earth where I sat. The watchers seemed to have comprehended what was happening but could do little more than comb the air blindly, hoping to hit one of us.

We reached the Traveler and the protectors and then were immediately back in my own valley at the little fire and in our regular forms. The Traveler was beaming.

"Well done! Take a few moments. Get solid. Draw this fire energy into you."

We followed his instructions, Red Feather taking a few careful draughts, me pulling quite a bit more. I looked at the mountains towering close above the valley and the blinding sunlight already on their peaks. A beautiful June day was rising. I thought about the Emeen and sent her some of that light.

32

Just a Celebration

Arrow had not mentioned whether our next meeting would be at the full or new moon. With the approach of the full moon I felt a pull and resolved to journey on the day it was exact.

In my valley it was another perfect alpine summer morning, crisp but not cold, beneath a cloudless sky. The Traveler was in his spot, leaning into an impossibly tiny fire, just a spark really, feeding it pine needles one by one. He looked up and winked. Today his appearance kept shifting rapidly from a near-toothless man of many seasons and the taller, younger shaman I was used to seeing. The effect was startling.

"Go. Take your protector," he said, ignoring my distraction. "Someone needs to keep this fire going." He feigned intense focus on his pine needles. Then as if in afterthought, he looked up again and said, "This is a beautiful place you have created."

Red Feather, the protector, and I journeyed to the same mountaintop as before. We could see watchers arrayed almost shoulder to shoulder across the cliff face where our cave door was concealed. A frontal approach by stealth or force seemed equally tedious, and we headed across the mountains to a fog bank that was moving in from the ocean. I was reminded that it was probably winter here, a time of fog and damp on this desert coast.

As we moved deeper into the mist we encountered the Amazonian and the African woman. They had the same thought we did, which was to let the fog carry us up the rocky valley. It would be slower, but nobody seemed in any haste. I was heartened to meet some Council members. I had been thinking that it might be good to get the names of all the others and took the opportunity to ask them. From the woman

I got something rather formal starting with Mrs. or Lady and was about to ask again when she cut me off sternly.

"For best invisibility one must shed all names!"

She was right of course. Her reminder brought me back to the fact that there was some real danger at hand. It seemed best to leave my protector as a decoy. With the others, Red Feather and I dispersed our forms and thoughts to become water droplets in fog. The on-shore breeze blew our cloud up the valley, scattering us even more until we were just wispy fingers of moisture moving past the watchers. We slowly penetrated the rock matrix, which felt more like pure will than stone, and gradually refocused our forms within.

At first it seemed the cave was dark and no one was home—not even the others from the fog bank—until I realized it was a function of my own lack of form. As I became fully materialized—if one can use the term for a projection of consciousness—I found that quite a few members were already present, including Arrow. Others were slowly coming into shape as well. There was a warmth of feeling and a sense of ease that made me very glad to have undertaken the journey.

Arrow spoke finally. "Welcome! I did not call you, nor was this some kind of test, but here you all are! This is wonderful. It shows the strength of the Council and your ability to connect. Excellent!" He was ebullient. "Let's party."

We held hands to harmonize. Silver light flooded our room on yet another full moon in June. There was a sweetness to it I did not recall from the last full-moon meeting.

As we were appreciating the living light, Arrow said, "There is no need to broadcast this light. Our Mistress sheds more than enough of her light on all. This is just a celebration!"

The slight tension in the cave evaporated and the silver intensified. We released our hands after a time, though the light remained constant.

"She does not radiate her own light," Arrow said softly, "yet she does! Where does it come from?" He stopped, struggling against sudden intoxication, then regained himself. "She is just like you. You are visible through reflected light, but you each have your own radiance as well. You can choose to shine—or not."

Motioning for us to join hands again, he said, "After the work of the solstice comes the moon of celebration. Yes, yes, I know what I said before, but this one just feels like a celebration." We sat in silence for a long time, enjoying our connection with each other, the Earth, the moon, allowing ourselves just a little pride in our efforts over the past months.

"The veils between the dimensions are so thin now," Arrow said at last. "Many things are being released into the world, both wonderful and horrible. Who is better qualified to deal with them than you? This is the work of our time." He peered about as he always did when he was about to make a big point.

"And yes, there was an energetic wave."

I was pleased to hear him say so, for in a figurative sense I was nearly swamped a few days prior.

"How could you miss it? Where did it come from?" He looked suspiciously at the cave roof from under his eyebrows as if expecting something to fall on his head. Everyone laughed. "How should I know? Where do ocean waves come from? Where does weather come from? It's not like a radio signal. That's more what we do. But remember that we are all floating in a great ocean, the ocean called space. There are waves all the time because our cosmic sea is not static. You're more aware of it now. What was it? I just don't know." He shrugged to more laughter. "But like a wave you can surf it, you can swim it, you could let it wash over you, or you could even drown. Sometimes you just have to hang on! Take your pick. One aspect is that after it has passed things can look a hell of a lot different. I'll leave you with something else: we all create waves. By ourselves just little ones, of course." I hoped he would continue, but he only laughed and fell silent, still smiling. We sat in the fullness of the moment.

Finally he broke the long silence. "Let us enjoy this time. Send light where you choose."

I did, sending it to loved ones, friends, pets, leaders—including those among the powerful who were less than beloved yet sorely in need of illumination—and then to parts of the planet. After some of our earlier work, it felt easy but no less important.

"Leave carefully," Arrow said when we had finished, adding in a stage whisper, "They aren't even sure we're here!"

Red Feather and I left as a mist, this time slowly sinking down the rock face behind the watchers. They seemed more agitated now, although their attention was still directed outward from the cliff. Several had detached themselves from the guard to patrol farther out. We moved slowly over the boulders on the valley floor, stopping in the shadows and blending with the fog that was now retreating under the growing heat of day. Reaching the diminishing cloudbank off shore, we lingered, gathering enough form for the protector to locate us. Whether another protector or watcher could have found us there, I do not know. But I did have some new thoughts about whom those watchers might work for. Certainly they didn't work for themselves. Arrow once said that we might be surprised at the answer. Now, if my ideas were at least partially correct, he was right.

We returned to my valley, where time seemed to have stopped during our adventure. The Traveler now stood before his little fire completely ignoring it. His form was the familiar one. He looked at us carefully.

"I will return in two days," he said, referring to our next session.

Having taken on a part-time job, I wasn't sure I could be ready. Two days hence was a workday. Whether I met him in the morning or the evening, it would make for a long day. I tried to negotiate. The Fourth of July holiday was just four days off. Why not then?

"No," he said, without amusement. "We need the full-moon energy. It will still be strong. Two days," he repeated, and faded out.

His teachings were powerful and enlightening, but sometimes I wished they came more slowly.

33

Courage

~July~
Moon in Leo, one day past new

It had been a hot night in what was now becoming a very hot summer. I awoke early, unrefreshed but unwilling to rise and abandon my discomfort. In the past few days, allegations had come my way in the outer world regarding certain teachers. The assertions questioned their integrity and purposes and were plausible enough in the way of good rumors to demand attention. My dreams were disturbing and obscure.

)

Two days before, spurred by those rumors and the people bearing them, I decided somewhat reluctantly to undertake a discreet investigation of the situation, journeying from my valley. I was surprised to find the Traveler waiting.

"I am going with you," he stated flatly.

At our destination, I observed things carefully and in stillness, noting with appreciation the rather artful first layer of defense. He suggested how I might proceed, but I had already seen enough. Although I still carried a new seed of caution, now I was more concerned about the rumor bearers and the source of their certainty than with the rumors.

I turned to the Traveler when were again in the valley. "Why did you come with me?"

"To restrain you."

I sensed approval that I had not taken his suggestion as an endorsement. How far would he have allowed me to go?

)

Today, I was glad once again to have Red Feather along for the journey. At the portal he seized one of the torches that blazed on either side and drew it through my field carefully.

"Cleansing," he explained.

I felt slightly more refreshed and we proceeded. The air seemed stagnant. The day would be hot there too. I gazed into my valley, wondering if the Traveler was present. We found he was not, yet his absence did nothing to reassure me. How was I to journey to the cave? I felt slow and stupid. Should I become an animal? How about a dragon? That would be something. I didn't feel at all like passing through rock or doing the dance around the watchers. In fact, the whole watcher business just seemed silly and tiresome. I sat down to gather strength.

Suddenly I was aware of Odínn's presence. This was highly unusual. Normally I went to meet him. He looked at me with his strong eye, rather like a bird, and then a smile appeared in his beard.

"Set your intent to arrive exactly where you sit—both of you."

Could it be that simple? Why hadn't we done this before? I usually enjoyed the journeying, but now the solution seemed easy and obvious. I stood again and with intent was at the cave, in place with Red Feather.

I do not know how many were there already or how the others arrived, for I was still working on maintaining my focus. At length I knew everyone was present. I looked up. Some were lost in thought. Arrow was casting his eyes over the assembly.

"Join hands. Harmonize!" he said at last and almost inaudibly.

We felt the violet light rise immediately. It bathed our cave and moved out to engulf the entire world. Holding the vision, we attuned to the light and to each other, retrieving the scattered pieces of ourselves from all the places we had left them. The mood seemed to improve and we finally released hands.

Arrow did not hesitate. "I told you the Earth is at a tipping point. It is one we share. The forces of inertia are arrayed against her, and us. This can come in many forms, not just the obvious and overt ones. There is also danger in the words of well-meaning friends and family beset by their own growing fears. You will be presented innuendo, told to be real, be realistic, face the facts — as they see them. But make no mistake: ultimately it is the powerful, ancient, living thought forms of culture and religion that oppose us. And why not? The alternatives and new ways are unknown. Even prophecy is over.

"What is required now is courage. We will bring up the yellow light." He looked around the room and read the question on several faces. "Yes, in some places yellow is associated with cowardice. Think about it! Before courage there is fear. It is visible in a person's aura. But how can courage exist without fear or cowardice? One defines the other, and courage can grow out of fear. You all have experienced this. Join hands. Focus on yellow, simply the color."

We followed his command and felt the color rise.

"Now source from the yellow ray, not yourselves," Arrow directed. "Don't worry where it comes from."

I opened outside myself and could feel an emanation of yellow light from an unknown place, like a beam of information or wisdom. Still, the light in our cave seemed to sputter and waver. "This is hard," I thought to myself, and wondered if we would go through all the colors and whether each would be just as difficult or more so than the last. I had thought violet would be the hardest.

"It *is* hard," Arrow said, without looking at me. "Last time we partied. Now we work!"

I looked around. Nobody was smiling. I realized this had less to do with our current difficulties as much as our personal experiences since the last meeting. Arrow's words were always on target. Motives and integrity were being twisted everywhere, as the archaic thought forms and masks — personal and planetary — sought to maintain their framework. It was going to get even more ugly.

"Give it a break," Arrow said sharply.

A sense of relief filled the room. Upstairs from my meditation space, my wife had made coffee. The scent was inviting. A fresh cup might be just the thing. Maybe I could get some and return.

"Now try again." Arrow's words returned my attention to the cave. "Yellow, not gold!"

The distinction might have been what we needed. We were able to bring up the yellow light more strongly and could sustain it, at least in the cavern.

As we held hands, Arrow spoke. "What is the ultimate source? *Your* source. Remember your divinity. Remember! That remembering, that source, is a sword! It cuts through all the thought forms arrayed against you, those forms that are yours and those that are put upon you."

The light now rose even more strongly. We felt it going out to inform the Earth, particularly our human race.

"This is especially for you," Arrow spoke again. "We need you to be sources of light and courage. When in doubt, remember! Remember your divine origin, your immortality, your direct connection to Spirit."

Red Feather was nodding in agreement. I recalled him telling me how his primary defense against sorcery was exactly such an affirmation.

I began to feel my third chakra, the energy center at the solar plexus, resonating and starting to pulse. At the same time I felt the yellow light pulsing through the planetary meridians and rising in all hearts as a whisper of remembrance—a reminder. I wondered how this yellow energy might manifest in some, because the third chakra is sometimes called the place of will and the warrior. Then I understood that if this energy was accepted and allowed to grow it would cut through all illusions of separation. What we offered was just a gift, exactly as Arrow had emphasized earlier.

We broke our circle. Unlike many of the other times there was no air of celebration. It felt more like quitting time at the office, though nobody moved to leave. I looked at Arrow and saw his eyes smile slightly.

"So," he exclaimed, "how in the world will you get home?" He looked perplexed and scanned us desperately, fooling no one. "You didn't arrive as luminous warriors, but you will leave that way—through the front door."

As he spoke, the cave entrance brightened to daylight. Those of us who didn't have their backs to the opening could see watchers gathering. One rushed the entrance, but Arrow simply flicked the back of his hand as if brushing off a troublesome insect and the shadow bounced away.

"Remembering our Source, holding our intent, we will all leave as luminous warriors. No scrambling. No enemies!"

We streamed from the cave and formed something of a wedge,

shooting over the valley to the opposite mountaintop, watchers trailing. Some of them attacked but seemed to rebound with added force. My primary awareness was of a strong connection to Spirit and that only I could sever it.

As we stood in a circle in the misty sunshine, Arrow said, "Your own thought forms of fear can be manipulated against you most cleverly. They can be tailored perfectly. Yet most often there is no specific direction against you. It is just the logic of consensus reality and perhaps your own unwitting complicity. I will leave you to consider this idea."

All around us the watchers frothed in pure fury, though none of us was engaging in any defensive effort. "Like howling savages from an old movie," I marveled. Clearly, these entities wanted our attention more than anything else.

Of our own accord we linked hands again, and brought up the yellow light, simply for the joy of manifestation, sending it out like a beacon.

"Well done," Arrow said finally. We meet again in one month. Time to talk about love!"

We dropped hands, noting indifferently as the watchers buzzed about like flies. Just the same, I was relieved that we were not meeting any sooner.

Red Feather and I dropped into the rock and returned to my valley. Odínn was still there. I asked about a dream from the previous night in which I had misplaced a yellow backpack containing some important sacred objects.

He smiled. "Courage!"

34

Harmony

The following month was eventful, not so much in terms of daily busyness but certainly in the events that take place within us all and on other levels as well. It was during this time that I had my encounter with Tezcatlipoca, the god of the smoking mirror. Soon thereafter, a moment came when I felt something I could only describe as deadness leave my body, allowing me to see a number of apparent certainties in much different light. The moment this occurred I happened to be facing west. As it did, a phrase came to me from an invocation I often use when opening sacred space in that direction.

> Mother-Sister Jaguar, show us the way
> beyond death and dying.
> Help us to leap cleanly across the Rainbow Bridge,
> leaving no enemies in this world or the next.

And I was reminded that Jaguar often has some things to say about clinging to only one perception.

I felt as if I was done with the dark dance that is sometimes mistaken for life. It was like stepping from a shadowy alley into sunshine. With this near-literal enlightenment there also came a few points of shame regarding my own complicity and some realizations about the nature of the earlier rumors and "friendly advice" that I had been receiving from another shaman. From this many other events flowed.

)

A few nights before the new moon, I awoke suddenly, certain of a massive psychic attack against my house. Red Feather was right there and may have been the one who roused me. On an impulse I had opened sacred space before going to sleep, something I rarely did. Now I was glad. After the initial jump to vigilance, I saw that events were already in full swing overhead. The house seemed to have no roof, just a great bubble of energy. Above the dome I could see my protector and other beings roaring about in pursuit of a number of watchers and dark forms. At the apex of the bubble, there was a great flaming sword swinging in burning arcs toward anything that made it past the protector and the other helpers. There were fireworks too. I knew the sword belonged to Archangel Michael, whom my wife often invoked. She slept peacefully on my right, and I made a note to thank her.

Relaxing, I watched the spectacular show with my mind's eye. It was astonishing and beautiful. Soon, however, I had a question. Who was behind this? I always had to know. Red Feather advised caution, but curiosity can be as great a motivator as fear. I left the safety of sacred space in the form of a strong power animal. The situation seemed complicated. The attackers and the psychic missiles came from different sources, most of which didn't appear to know me personally. Some were not even of our dimension. Yet I could identify several others whose source I did know. That no longer surprised me.

The subtlety with which friendly ties were manipulated was truly artful. I had certainly begun to doubt some key teachers and their motives, which of course raised questions about my own abilities to perceive. Once one holds another in suspicion, almost any word or deed can be ascribed to ulterior motive. As I looked back I realized that the rising doubts had begun almost a year before, June to be exact. There was a hiatus for most of the past month, which I later realized coincided with my friend's lengthy trip to another country. It was also during this time that I saw the deadness leave my body.

Soon after our contact resumed I found myself feeling slightly panicky without knowing why. I quickly checked the source. It was my friend, but I tracked immediately beyond to something not on the material plane. When I asked Odínn why he had not alerted me, he said I needed to discover things for myself. In addition, he said there was nothing I could do for my friend other than disengage and send love and light.

I worked quietly and carefully to sever all ties. In fact I was grateful for the teaching. As soon as I began, I received a strange message from the friend stating that because of his work during that foreign trip he was essentially invisible and could no longer be tracked. Further, because his veils had been lifted he could now see the veils in others. So, my efforts had been noted with alarm and probably triggered the night's festivities. Ultimately something didn't want me walking my path, which included work with the Council.

Now, my protector rushed to me and I joined the fray with gusto.

The animal that allowed me to assume its form seemed a real surprise to the attackers. Some of its tricks had surprised me too the only other time I merged with it. Nor had I told anyone aside from my wife.

At length another fine idea occurred to me. Why not capture one of the watchers? I sent the idea to my protector who responded instantly with what almost felt like a warm thought. As a watcher hurtled toward us, we moved off as if in panic then wheeled and caught it in a net of light. The protector wrapped itself around all three of us for invisibility as I tightened the net mercilessly.

"Whom do you serve?" I demanded. The net seemed to cause it real pain, but I kept tightening it, repeating my question. Its form became more and more evident, like a man of shadow and smoke but not nearly the size of my protector. Finally our captive relented.

"I will show you," it said, and I saw a cord stretching out of sight into the void.

I can only say I traced that cord carefully and with as much invisibility as I could muster, past a human master of worldly power and considerable talent as a sorcerer, to a dark figure beyond him, residing on a plane or dimension I didn't know. And though he knew I saw him, I looked beyond and saw that even he ultimately drew on God or Spirit. Can I say that I then entered the presence of God? I will. We talked as we did once before. He told me how Light and Dark define each other at many levels but that ultimately there is only Light. He allowed me to taste the suffering of the victim, to revel in the cruelty of the victimizer, and to touch the self-deception of the rescuer. I saw how each of us has been all those things and understood the purpose. Then he confirmed something I had once heard. "Above" him there is Another, although I couldn't really understand. We had a laugh. Mostly I was content to simply be in the white light that was all I could really see of him.

I finally followed that cord back down to the dark form. He let me pass unafraid and ultimately back to my house. Who or what was that figure? It is complicated, but it would be highly inaccurate to call it the Devil.

The battle was long over. Had anybody won? The protector still guarded our captive. Forming my intent into a blade, I severed the cord and watched one end snake into the distance while the other writhed for a moment and then withered to nothing.

"He is now yours to command," my protector said.

I liked that idea. It was all so like the Arabian Nights. Even though I already had a genie of sorts, here was one I had caught myself. A trophy! A magic slave! Then I had a better idea.

"If I release him, whom will he serve?" I asked.

"Himself, or whoever he chooses."

Using the blade, I sliced the net around the captive, saying, "You are free to do as you will as long as you do no harm."

It seemed to look at me and then moved off slightly, regarding us.

"Thank you. I won't forget," it said finally. Then it arced off as if it had just remembered joy. I felt as if I had passed a test.

"It was the right thing to do," the protector said.

"What if I had kept it?" I asked.

"Acceptable. No blame. But this is better."

"But here you are now," I said. "Do you wish to be freed too?"

"I am here by choice."

I understood that part of his choice stemmed less from a desire to help a human than to further his own evolution in some way. Still, I was touched.

There was a lot to ponder, which occupied me until the next Council meeting.

)

It was early evening in the valley. Red Feather and I stood at our usual place on the rim and saw a campfire below. Above us the mountain peaks still glowed pink, but Jupiter was already bright in the south. It occurred to me that Michael is associated with Jupiter, or perhaps it was another sign from the Traveler. We made our way to meet him.

"Much has changed for you," he said to me without rising as we approached. "Things you thought were true are untrue. You have learned how the slow drip of poison feels in your heart. And you have worked to undo it without rancor. That is good." He turned to Red Feather. "I commend you on your restraint!"

"It was not easy." Red Feather looked at me sympathetically but without his usual humor.

It seemed that I was the only one who hadn't figured things out. Even my wife had broken her long silence about the matter. I felt like a child caught in one of those "teachable moments." Well, I had been taught.

"I will journey with you," said the Traveler. "And your protector."

Then we were on the mountaintop across from the cave. The dusk there had advanced almost into night. We could make out two things: the brightly lit cave with a single, tiny figure seated inside, and a series of watchers arrayed against us as densities in the growing dark, motionless.

Council members had begun joining us, suddenly present without actually seeming to appear. The mood was festive. Had everyone faced something similar in the last week? I began with a few handshakes but soon was hugging everybody.

Alice gave me a kiss on the lips.

Paqo gripped my hands and looked into my eyes. "Hermano."

"You should come to my house, I need another husband!" the African lady said.

"I already have a wife," I replied, unsure whether she meant a husband in addition to one she now had or just a replacement.

"I'm sure she's a good woman and wouldn't mind sharing," she answered, laughing along with those closest to us.

The European woman who usually sat between Alfred and Amáne told me her name was Edwina and that she was from the British Isles, which reminded me that I still didn't know everyone's name.

I resolved again to start asking, but forgot my resolution when Amáne hugged me warmly immediately thereafter. I did find out that Victoria was Swedish but not of my training, she was quick to say.

We all turned to face the cave. The situation was not lost on anyone. I hesitated but then felt called to step forward.

"I offer to lead."

Heads nodded, and Red Feather and I moved out slowly over the void. Behind us the Council members formed a line two abreast with the Amazonian last, followed by a number of protectors. I noted with some curiosity that ours were all somewhat bigger than the ones we were facing. As we approached their solid line, I held up my right hand. Wordlessly the watchers parted, formed a corridor, and then seemed to kneel as we passed. We entered the cave. The watchers remained where they were, while our protectors assumed position at the entrance. Arrow stared into a large fire that was more gold than green and said nothing.

As soon as we were seated, he seized my hand and then Victoria's, motioning everyone to do the same. A white light came up strongly, overwhelming the light of the fire. It was almost tangible, so dense I could barely see across the cave, and well beyond the intensity of any white light we had encountered before. Within it was something more powerfully unifying than our circle of hands. We sustained it — or it sustained us — for a long time until Arrow broke the ring and the light subsided. It took a few moments for him to speak.

"The White Light," he said softly, almost in awe. "A door is open, informing us and the planet." He fell silent again, as if the experience was entirely new to him.

The white continued to ebb slowly until only gold-green firelight remained. How long had we been here? The thought was simultaneous to us all, and people began to stir.

I could no longer contain a question that had long been marinating.

"At the outset you stated that the proper relation between humans and Earth is one of reciprocity. But we have been working beyond reciprocity as we bring light. What is our proper relation to Mother Earth?"

"Ah!" Arrow turned toward me curiously and then turned to eye the Council. "It always begins and ends there, but our proper relation now is to help her give birth to herself. Those visions you hold help her to move forward in her difficult time — her time of crisis. Again I must remind you that you are holding them, not imposing them. Many now seek to save her. Very noble. But from what? Change? It is well under-way. Of course she is burdened, yet they are in fear just as much as those who are locked in their anger and hatred. Part of it is a fear of scarcity. Hear this: fear is her larger burden. Our work here is to find the new dream that pulls her forward." He fell silent.

Alfred asked a question. "Where is this door that has opened? What is it?"

Arrow's laugh was sudden but not unkind. "You don't know? You! All of you! You are the doors. Together, we are a door." He gave us an infectious grin.

"As I keep saying, we are at the end of prophecy. The great Olmec timekeepers and visionaries and those who sustained parts of that wis-dom after their demise could not see past the long period ending a few years from now. It would be interesting to know if they could even see the beginning of this new period," he added somewhat to himself, then redirected his attention to us. "Some of them called it the end of time. What they meant was that it is the end of a particular kind of time. The door that is opening is the time to come. Humans and the Earth will source from a new destiny and a new self-vision. You and many others are the doors. It has begun."

His head snapped toward me. "Are you getting all this? Write it down!"

I laughed with the others.

We joined hands and the White Light came up instantly, this time moving out of our cave to inform the Earth, running through the plan-etary meridians, strengthened by the huaca that was always active at our crystal mountain. It suffused the globe, and extended many miles into space. I felt Earth shiver beneath me in my meditation but was unable to tell what I was experiencing.

"Keep holding!" Arrow shouted from far off. "Keep holding!" which he repeated this continually as we sustained the energy much longer than usual. Finally he allowed us to release our hands, though the White Light diminished only slightly.

"Return to this vision daily, hourly. This is very important," he said.

Following a brief rest, we reformed the circle, this time using the light to push the great crust of dark thought forms out from the globe.

When the momentum we had imparted failed, they came rushing back like an oily wave. Without direction from Arrow, we held the orb of light around the planet, though it might be more accurate to say that we informed it. The wave broke and spread across the white globe in enormous rancid smears that swallowed it for a few long seconds before slowly transforming into the White Light itself and feeding it. We began drawing more darkness out of the planet and transforming that too.

"Enough!" Arrow said at last. "There is much unfinished business, but this is a start. Return to this particular vision too. Now take a rest."

I was glad to stop. It almost seemed that we were moving too fast.

Arrow was in high spirits now. "What about love? I know it's a question that has arisen for some of you. Well," he said lowering his voice to draw us in, "love is a many-splendored thing!" and laughed at his own reference. "Love is all you need." He laughed again, then feigned seriousness. "Anyway, who wrote the book of lu-uv?" He was on a roll. The specific references to ancient pop songs were lost on a number of Council members, but they understood what he was doing and smiled with the others. He got hold of himself and said, "There is a whole ball of confusion here."

I braced for a new onslaught of pop lyrics, but it seemed that was the last.

"Many things are called love and have at least a piece of it," he went on. "Perhaps it is best just to look to compassion for its purest expression because everything else that is called love contains an element of attachment. There is a thing just beyond love that is called harmony. What we really seek is to find harmony in its deepest sense, as a great harmonic chord that contains everything and its opposite in balance."

He left us to ponder for a little before announcing, "Time to leave!"

Nobody made a move, mostly from fatigue.

I glanced around and then announced, "I can lead."

"Excellent," Arrow declared. "Little Feather and Red Feather, the Feather Brothers!"

At the cave mouth, which had been closed during our session, the seamless rock evaporated, revealing our protectors still on guard. Beyond them the watchers stood in ranked silence. I noted again how they looked like smoky men, though now I also saw a fiery center.

"They really are jinn," I thought to myself. In the same formation as before, we moved toward the mountain where we had begun. Arrow followed, and we formed a circle at the summit. I turned toward the watchers who now followed at a distance and said. "Join us!" Our protectors formed a loose ring around our circle and the watchers formed a circle beyond that. We humans joined hands again and brought up a little of the White Light, holding it without effort before allowing it to recede. Overhead the Perseid meteors had begun their show. I was tired and had no idea how I would return to my valley without being followed. A thought came to me, and as nobody else seemed to be moving, I turned to the watchers.

"You are all free to choose whom you serve — or serve no one."

Fire came up in each of them. There was silence and then a sudden rushing noise as they shot off in different directions, echoing the Perseids. Were they indeed free? So it seemed. Some time might have passed, but just as suddenly there was no one left on the mountain but Red Feather, Arrow, my protector, and the Traveler who had appeared from nowhere. Arrow turned to Red Feather and me.

"I know of your work — both of you," he said quietly. "It is well done."

I appreciated his words, for the past year had been one of doubt.

"Take them home," Arrow said to the Traveler. "They are tired."

We were back at the fire in my valley. Jupiter had barely moved.

Raising his arm toward the brilliant planet, the Traveler said, "Draw on his energy. Let it refresh you."

Red Feather and I inhaled the light deep into our bodies, allowing it to fill us.

"Now the real work begins," observed the Traveler.

35

Red

~September 11~
New Moon in Virgo

As soon as Red Feather and I stepped through the door into the valley we smelled smoke. We looked at each other and laughed. The Traveler. It was a fresh mountain morning, only now the air had a slight chill that spoke of autumn. The summer days were relentlessly hot where I lived, the hottest on record, as they said almost every year now. I was glad for the promise of coolness. Yet what got my attention was the realization that a long time had passed since I had smelled something here without making a conscious effort. A faint sense of inadequacy washed over me.

The Traveler was very much there, along with a roaring fire. As we approached, he seized a smoldering piece of wood from the fire's edge and immediately began smudging Red Feather. Then he thrust the brand back into the flames for a few moments and started on me. He frowned, dropped the wood, and seized another whose end was burning fiercely. He turned to me again, saying, "You always forget your back and store much heaviness there."

"I know."

"This will help." He went at his task with thoroughness. Finally, placing the entire piece into the fire center, he shook his hands out as if they were wet to release whatever might have clung to him.

"Bring your protector," he said, looking up.

"Why, don't you have one?" I asked in challenge.

"Don't know. Don't seem to have one today," he grinned, and once again we were at the mountaintop across the valley from the Crystal Cave. The morning there was just as beautiful, though it felt more like spring. In the clear air we could see the ocean in the far distance.

Red

The watchers were also there. I counted twelve. In the time since the events of the last Council meeting, I was aware of their presence at several ceremonial fires. They brought a slight heaviness that a few people attending remarked, but only after the first fire did I understand what was happening. Their presence was not threatening, nor did they interfere. I began to welcome them as guests, though it was hard for me to determine if they were there to protect or just liked a good fire. Now they ringed the mountain. As Red Feather and I proceeded across the valley they flanked us left and right like an honor guard. It was such a fine day I almost preferred to stay outside.

Inside, Arrow and Victoria were the only ones present. Why did I still have trouble remembering her name? An orange fire burned in the center. I focused on it while they conversed in low tones. This was a new color. Arrow turned to me.

"Welcome." He bowed his head slightly and then appraised me for a moment. "What you have been doing is impressive. To meet the Dark One and to step outside of fear and attraction, and then to sit in God's presence... Impressive!"

)

My encounter of the previous month did not end on that particular night. A few days later the Dark One came to me in my inner world in hideous form. I was unafraid and instead told him, or it, that unless he assumed a more reasonable aspect I would simply refuse to deal with him. He complied and then said he would return in several days but only once more, for it took great effort to visit me in such a place. In the meantime I spoke with Odínn.

"He is right," Odínn said. "It is almost beyond his ability to come to you here."

"What should I do?"

"Do as you wish. He appreciates your nonjudgment and wishes to find a way of engagement. But before doing so, it might be good to connect with your male and female shadows again. It's been awhile!"

My guest did return, stating again that it was the last time he could meet me there but that he would like to work with me — not toward any goal or dark end, but simply at a place of common ground beyond duality. And I agreed, not because I sought power but because I saw the way of it and how Light and Dark define each other within Unity. For several days thereafter I experienced a strange sense of weightlessness. I had no idea how things would proceed, but it felt as if some kind of truce was in effect.

)

Now, at the Crystal Cave, Arrow continued. "This is why you sit on my left and she sits on my right. You have wondered, haven't you? Well, you engage the Dark. You have stepped beyond judgment to compassion."

I wasn't so sure. "It would have been easier just to engage the Light," I replied.

He laughed, nodding toward Victoria. "You can ask her about that!"

Others were arriving. When all were present, we each made eye contact all around. To Emeen, on my left, I said, "May the grace and peace of the Prophet be upon you."

She beamed. "And upon you!"

As we exchanged these words, I felt a spark of light and love fall on us as if a doorway had opened for a moment.

Arrow directed us to join hands. We brought up the White Light easily to surround and permeate the Earth. It had a thick consistency, rather like milk, completely masking the orange firelight before receding. We released the circle and held silence for a few moments.

"Time for the red light," Arrow announced without smiling. As he said so, the fire slowly moved from orange to red, casting us all in a color that seemed foreign. "In many ways this is harder," he said. "Perhaps because it is all too familiar." He looked around, then added softly, "But it must be done."

We focused on the fire color and brought it up slowly and with difficulty. It was hard to sustain and somewhat uncomfortable. After a time we relaxed. The red light dropped intensity but lingered, almost sticky.

Across the room, Alice spoke. "Why?"

"As I said, a lot of people have ideas about how to heal the Earth, or how to change her—what they think she best needs. We have held our own visions, but now we will take a step back. And as I keep saying, we are here to help her change—whatever she chooses. This light is part of her process. We will sustain her as she enters this difficult phase in a way that does not bring unnecessary destruction. Remember your true natures and origins. We are not all from the same place, but none of us is from here. Everyone on Earth is a participant in this change. Many are here just as mouths—hungry mouths, greedy mouths—so many! But all are part of the process. Bring up the red!"

It came up strongly this time, like an angry volcano. Each of us *was* a volcano, and Earth was surrounded by thick, red light that also began to course through the planetary meridians like fiery blood. I was surprised to see that it came as something of a relief to our planet. She had been holding back for so long. A great serpent filled our cavern until there was nothing but compressed coils. It suddenly shot out into the world as powerful, formative energy, leaving the space filled completely with red fire and the echo of a long-suppressed roar.

A lengthy silence followed, as the fire receded to the center of the cave.

"Once again, the date of our meeting is not a coincidence," Arrow said.

I could see that several people didn't immediately understand the reference, but most nodded. The date was now a talisman in my country. "Those events were a trigger," he continued. "It is still unfolding in human consciousness, unwinding that red energy."

There was another long silence. Then, without prompting, we joined hands and brought up the red light strongly. This time it was less cloudy and angry, and we could sense relief in our Mother Earth. That she had held it for so long could only have come from great love. Slowly the light faded and we finally broke the circle. It had been work.

"After our last time there was an 8.0 earthquake," someone said.

"Yes, but we must give her our permission and hold her in safety while she enters this phase," Arrow replied sharply. "It could not have happened any sooner. Work with this red light as you have with the White," and he nodded toward Alice.

The doorway lightened and daylight streamed in as if nothing had happened. I was glad that no volcanoes had sprouted during our meeting. Nobody spoke and soon people began to leave. I waited until the first to arrive were the last to leave and went with Victoria across the valley to the mountaintop. The watchers joined us as soon as we exited and again formed a circle around the summit.

"It seems you have many friends," she observed.

"So it seems."

"We are all grateful."

I looked past her and saw a guide figure with a protector.

"I do not know you, but I look forward to the day we meet in the outer world," I said.

"As do I." She turned and was gone.

In my valley, the Traveler was at his fire. He smudged us again thoroughly. Red Feather smiled at me and we rose up to meet the bright day.

36

Sacred Fire

-October-
New Moon in Libra

The morning spoke of a brilliant autumn day, but when Red Feather and I pushed into the valley it was crisp night. We were in the night to come.

"How odd," I thought. Usually Council journeys occurred almost in real time.

At the valley rim, we saw the Traveler's fire and joined him, collecting the protector and Aquila along the way. He stood, stepped forward, and kissed me on both cheeks. I was surprised. Then he turned, held Red Feather's shoulders, and brought his head close to either side of Red Feather's. It seemed to be a familiar mode of greeting to my friend, for I could feel his warmth of appreciation. Resuming his seat, the Traveler motioned for us to sit. He passed a stick across to me.

"You have created a fire that is fueled by prayer." Then he handed one to Red Feather.

He referred to a three-day vigil fire from which my wife and I had just returned. It was an unexpectedly powerful experience. We prayed for our Earth and the beings on it and found the fire to be a strong teacher. When it finally reached the end of its life, no amount of additional fuel could sustain it. Those of us who were there performed a short version of the death rites for it but not before bringing it into our medicine bundles and our hearts. During our return, we were aware of the fire continuing to burn on some other plane as well as our power to access its vitality.

Red Feather and I blew prayers into our sticks for that fire and for the Earth's continuing transformation in ease and beauty, placing them carefully in the flames. The Traveler handed me another.

197

"This one is for you."

I placed a prayer in it for remembrance of everything I was about to experience. We watched the sticks smolder, flare, and then quickly dissolve into white-hot ash.

"Let's journey," the Traveler exclaimed as if the idea had just come to him and standing in one movement.

We were on the mountain opposite the Crystal Cave. A dense sea fog was rolling up the stony valley, but across the way I could see a fire. I was aware of jinn, many of them, surrounding us without threat. Red Feather and I made our way over to the cave. A regular fire much like the one we had just left burned unattended. We took our place and began to feed it the good thoughts and prayers that came to us. Soon others arrived and joined us in the tending. The only empty place was Arrow's, but no one was alarmed as we exchanged smiles and greetings from the heart.

Suddenly Arrow was there with a wide smile.

"You can all sustain the fire on your own now," he said. "It burns in your hearts and thoughts. Over the last month you have sustained the red light. It has not been easy, has it?"

A few shook their heads. No it had not. I gave it quite a bit of effort during my meditations and felt constant resistance. It was hard to determine the source, for it seemed personal, collective, and planetary at once.

"Your personal changes mirror the larger sphere," Arrow continued. "That is the way of it now."

He allowed us to take in his words before declaring, "Harmonize!"

We could feel the energy of each Council member meshing and then flowing. I recognized instantly that this was the energy I had felt over the past month and that it was strengthened.

"Bring up red light," Arrow commanded. We did so, maintaining it with relative ease, though the fire retained its original color. "It is a strong, transformational energy," he said finally. "One we don't use often because it is harder to sustain."

Without prompting, we saw the Earth surrounded by red light again. Returning my focus to the fire, I saw our planet in its center burning like a pinecone full of resin. I was startled. Looking closer I could see that the fire was consuming a thick, pitchy outer layer while the blue beauty within was untouched.

"The dark thought forms are burning!" Arrow said triumphantly. "This is part of our continuing work."

We broke the circle and watched transfixed as the pinecone Earth flared.

"Feed the fire with your bright thoughts and prayers," Arrow said at length. "Blow!"

We leaned in and the fire leaped but continued to burn steadily.

"Remember this," he continued. "Thoughts are things, both light and dark. Each has an effect, but the dark ones are heavier. At the outset, we were opposed by the momentum of the dark forms and those who serve them. It has not stopped, but now you have a deeper understanding. Fear feeds them. Our Earth is shedding them. She has a fever. Look at her burn! But there is a bright future for her and for the humans. Let us not burden her process by adding layers of our own desires for an outcome, or our fears. Instead, lend her your visions. Then hold space for her transformation—and ours—to something greater than any can imagine." He stopped, leaned in, and looked at each of us carefully.

"Honor the Dark, not by fear but by acknowledgment, recognition, and compassion. It is just the same as with the shadow work you have all done in one way or another. Your shadow cannot be killed or ignored. In fact, a brighter light will cast a darker shadow. But with recognition, that shadow can be a powerful creative force." He leaned back as if to relax.

"Bring up the Black Light!"

We jumped. It seemed such a long time since we had done so, but the Black Light came up easily, swirling around our cave like living shadow.

"Now bring up gold!"

This was an even older one. It came up just as easily, but more much more powerful and more metallic than so long ago. Gold joined swirling black in our cave before entering the fire. We watched as the fire tipped between black and gold until there was equilibrium. Both were present and active in beautiful flame without overwhelming the other.

The Earth was gone.

Arrow allowed us time to take in what we had witnessed. The fire continued in its perfect state—a wonderful fire.

"The fire storm has passed, and we have completed a step," he said at last. "After one step comes another. But the next will not be recorded." He turned to face me and his unwavering gaze entered mine. "Send these words out."

I nodded and there was silence until someone—I couldn't tell whom—asked, "What about the other colors?"

"We will work with all twelve of them," Arrow smiled knowingly. A long silence reigned, as we considered the closing of one chapter and the verge of a new one.

"This fire now burns continuously," Arrow said at last, "because you sustain it in your thoughts. Let it teach you! Now take some and sustain it within your light-bodies."

People began reaching in and bringing living fire out to various energy centers and places in their bodies using cupped hands. I brought fire into my heart center, then the crown, and finally the base of my spine. At last Red Feather reached past me, took a pinch, and swallowed it. He looked around as if slightly confused and then suddenly lit up like a light bulb. Everyone laughed.

"See you next moon," Arrow said, and then vanished. The rest of us lingered. It felt the like last day of school, the trepidation and uncertainty of a long-ago first day now replaced by a sense of ease, familiarity, and even a feeling of mastery. Another first day would come, but not today.

Red Feather and I finally departed. We crossed over the canyon to the opposite mountain. The Traveler was there taking in the stars, now unobscured by fog.

"What a night," he said, absorbed. We looked up too. I saw we were again surrounded by beings. There were jinn, yet now they seemed to be just one ring within many rings of souls, all kneeling quietly with their attention on us. The Traveler ceased his stargazing and focused on me with a look of curiosity. I turned to him and then toward the great circle. Reaching into my heart center, I took a tiny seed of the living fire and blew over it continuously toward the assembly, moving clockwise. As I completed the circuit, there was a rush and we were alone again.

The fire in my valley still burned brightly on our return. We offered it more sticks, feeding its spirit with love.

"What a night," the Traveler said again.

And Then?

It is only with the heart that one can see rightly;
what is essential is invisible to the eye.

— Antoine de St. Exupéry

So, what happened? As I prepared this book and returned to words that in some cases I had not seen since I recorded them, the question kept presenting itself. I put it to Arrow.

"Everything and nothing," he answered, grinning. "From one perspective, nothing has changed at all. From another it has all changed. Nobody celebrates or mourns what didn't seem to happen. That is the nature of activating possibility: when you turn down a different street it is the only one you see. Its course seems straight." He laughed. "But we do get to choose. Three steps down that street, people forget that they were at a fork and made a choice. And when it comes to possibilities, it only takes a few holding simple intent for highest and best to activate something that might seem wildly improbable."

What I present here is only what I have been directed to record, which Arrow once told me is part of the transformation we all share. He said that simply by reading these words, you have participated in the work of uplifting the world.

The Council continues to meet and will do so until one of its members passes away. At that time its work will be complete. Whether one seed goes forth to begin another council or there are more seeds is beyond my ability to see. I do know there are other councils, both within our time line and outside of it, and that their work also continues. It has always been so. Perhaps you will form your own vision circle.

)

One of our greatest apprehensions is that we cannot allow our own spiritual authority. For millennia we have experienced that authority as primarily external and punishing, having ceded our primacy through laziness or fear. Suggesting otherwise has often entailed terrible consequences. History is laden with examples of suppression towards ones labeled heretic, infidel, healer, or shaman—entirely at the hands of fellow humans. Our task now is to transcend these fears. We are infinite and powerful, inseparably connected to all things within the unified consciousness that is Spirit. It is our birthright to know and experience this truth.

Some find it disturbing to discover there are human-created thought forms at every level from the personal to the planetary. They appear to exist apart from ourselves because we have given them power to create suffering and a sense of separation. We are good at creation, conscious and unconscious. But accepting our spiritual authority confers knowledge, responsibility, and the capacity to recognize the nature of such things. That acceptance gives us equal power to deal with what seems truly frightening through grace and harmony.

Encountering panic or the sense of threat, I return to Red Feather's advice that affirming a connection to Spirit is the best defense. It gives me courage to turn and face what induces fear from a place of clarity and stillness rather than an instinct to defend the ego. I also affirm the existence of a cadre of spiritual helpers eagerly waiting for each of us to become aware of their kind and loving presence. We are never alone or cut off, but we must choose to ask for their help and advice. Then be sure to say thank you!

)

In the vision circle I found it is possible to dream a new world into being. We did not proceed by weaving our well-intentioned but distorted notions of peace, love, God, or goodness into its fabric. Those unexamined notions too are fueled by unconscious old patterns and can be just as great a weariness as the notions we set them against. Rather, we brought pure light of Spirit into simple visions, unburdened by wounding or judgment and without regard for specific outcome. Then we let it inform our hearts and consciousness as a direct experience of joy and wonder. That teaching has been for me one of the great gifts of the Council.

Many see the world as a dangerous, hurtful place. Yet each of us has made a conscious choice to be here. Accepting ourselves as luminous beings doesn't mean we only need to hang on until someone drops us a ladder. It means we look down at our feet, notice that there is no distance between them and the ground, and then understand that we are conduits between heaven and Earth at a pivotal point. What a wonderful time to be alive!

Recently, Arrow emphasized again to me that in times of apprehension and transition it is important to hold an energizing, affirmative personal vision of a planetary future. "How exactly one gets there is a mystery, but people need to know they can do this and that it will pull them forward," he said. For me it continues to be the simple image of drinking pure water from a mountain stream. I can taste it. The water is cold and sweet, which it is a good sign that so many wonderful things would have conspired for it to be so. For you it might be the image of a smiling child being fed where there is now famine, or a Siberian tiger roaming fearless and wild.

I wish for this book to bring you hope. May you remember yourself as a divine being, co-creator of a living Universe that unfolds in every moment. May your every step be in beauty. Look within. Learn to trust the eyes of your heart. Hear its voice. It speaks truth to you, if you will listen. Then give it a vision.

Prologue

I Stood on a Hill

~ December 31 ~
New Moon in Capricorn

In a dream I stood on a hill with God, overlooking the City of Life. The cardinal gates were open wide, a spring wind kept the pennants on the walls moving, and there was much coming and going.

God said, "You people take things far too seriously."

When God speaks with language, it is difficult to follow what he says. Each word has its own power and exists simultaneously in all its forms, all its meanings, down to the original sound echoing back to the beginning of the universe. The letters in a written language themselves come alive. And of course there are the other languages within which a word or sound may also have meaning. So when he said "people" it came to me in every sense at once, my family, my nation, my culture, all humanity, not to mention all meanings as a verb and other forms. I had to agree that most of the people in the City of Life were going about things with desperate seriousness.

The famous Islamic tradition, attributed to God, came to mind: *I was a hidden treasure and wanted to be known.*

God laughed. "That's exactly right. I stand in awe of this treasure I have created."

I felt his sense of cosmic wonder and joy at the perfect unfoldment of an endlessly faceted, eternally expanding creation.

"Are you then the clockmaker god, standing apart and admiring his own work?" I asked.

He snorted. "That is a conception from an age of clockmakers. I am fundamental to everything," but he did not elaborate.

205

"You are gods yourselves, you know," He said after a bit, knowing my thoughts before they came to me. "Fairly high up in the scheme of things, actually, though most of you have forgotten. When you touch that knowledge, you find that nothing really matters—at least not in the way people like to think it does." He laughed at the great joke he had played on himself and then exclaimed, "Beautiful day!"

I seized the opportunity. "What about "bad"? By this I meant everything we humans think of as being un-good.

"I created that too. Interesting isn't it? It's co-eval with good."

My mind lit up with the coincidence of "eval" with "evil" and spun into what every English-speaker knows: evil is also "live" spelled backwards. I felt his pleasure that I got the cosmic pun.

He continued: "But bad isn't really that big an issue, not even as much an issue as good. That particular duality is hardly worth all the effort that goes into it and certainly not as a useful basis for organizing one's lives.

"I'm thinking of writing a book," I said.

"Excellent idea! I'll help."

Author: www.JeffFarwell.com

Passageway books, audio, and electronic editions are
available through bookstores, online retailers, and
directly from our website.

Passageway Publishing
PO Box 520411
Salt Lake City UT 84152

Email: orders@PassagewayPublishing.com
Web: www.PassagewayPublishing.com

PASSAGEWAY

Forthcoming!

JOURNEYMAN

ON THE SHAMAN'S PATH
WITH THE TRAVELER

Jeff Farwell

Available May 2010

www.PassagewayPublishing.com

Breinigsville, PA USA
27 August 2009
223094BV00001B/7/P